I'm not aware of too many things.
I know what I know if you know what I mean.

What I am is what I am.
Are you what you are or what?

- Edie Brickell, 1986

I Just Wanna Ride

(FTW)

I JUST WANNA RIDE

(FTW)

By

Robert R. Kopp

Black Oak
MEDIA

I Just Wanna Ride (FTW)

Cover and interior design by Michael Kleen

First Edition Spring 2012

ISBN-13: 978-1-61876-002-9

Published by Black Oak Media, Inc.

To order copies of this book contact:

Black Oak Media, Inc.
Rockford, Illinois
www.blackoakmedia.org
orders@blackoakmedia.org

Printed in the United States of America.

Dedicated with thanks to family, friends, and foes who prayed, prodded, and plagued me to be authentic!

Authenticity

The Skin Horse had lived longer in the nursery than any of the others. He was so old that his brown coat was bald in patches and showed the seams underneath, and most of the hairs in his tail had been pulled out to string bead necklaces. He was wise, for he had seen a long succession of mechanical toys arrive to boast and swagger, and by-and-by break their mainsprings and pass away. He knew that they were only toys, and would never turn into anything else. For nursery magic is very strange and wonderful, and only those playthings that are old and wise and experienced like the Skin Horse understand all about it.

"What is real?" asked the Rabbit one day.

"Does it mean having things that buzz inside you and a stick-out handle?"

"Real isn't how you are made," said the Skin Horse.

"It's a thing that happens to you. When a child loves you for a long, long time, not just to play with, but REALLY loves you, then you become Real."

"Does it hurt?"

"Sometimes." For he was always truthful.

"When you are Real you don't mind being hurt."

"Does it happen all at once, like being wound up, or bit by bit?"

"It doesn't happen all at once. You become. It takes a long time. That's why it doesn't often happen to people who break easily, or who have sharp edges, or who have to be carefully kept. Generally, by the time you are Real, most of your hair has been loved off, and your eyes drop out and you get loose in the joints and very shabby."

"But these things don't matter at all, because once you are Real you can't be ugly, except to people who don't understand."

- Margery Williams, *The Velveteen Rabbit* (1922)

Dr. Robert Kopp is no doubt an authentic biker who has experienced the adventure of being on two wheels for many years. "*FTW*" is a fascinating read that not only provides road worthy tips and great stories but also uses religions passages to draw parallels between Kopp's everyday biker life and his road to redemption. Dr. Kopp is no Saint by any means, as a matter of fact he is/was an extremely hardcore biker who lived fast and reckless for many years. His stories and journey to enlightenment are as authentic as his passion for the open road. Now the word "religion" may scare some people however there's no doubt that riding is a spiritual experience. Regardless of your denomination "*FTW*" is a one of a kind read that anyone who enjoys the freedom of riding will enjoy.

- Jay Barbieri, *American Thunder* &
Author of the *"Bikers Handbook"*

Contents

Forwards

I picked up an advance copy of Robert R. Kopp's latest book, *I Just Wanna Ride (FTW)*, with some serious misgivings. The author and I are worlds apart in both religion and lifestyle, and what could a Midwest pastor know about today's motorcycle scene, anyway?

That'll teach me to be so closed-minded. You'd think I'd know better, as many years ago I left the small town where I was born and raised, partially because of the narrow-mindedness I encountered there. Interestingly enough, Bob grew up in the same small town. We attended the same schools at the same time and hung out with the same people, and in an astounding turn of events we have re-connected some 40 years later. Once lost and now found? Amazing! Or providential, as Bob likes to say.

When I saw the subtitle *FTW*, I thought, well, at least he knows the lingo. But it goes deeper than that. FTW, the best-known biker-world acronym for Fuck The World, is Bob's attention-getting device to explain his views on being authentic. The book drew me in as it became clear that Bob's ability to dig beneath the surface of the motorcycling subculture enables him to draw parallels between bikers and the church, using anecdotes as well as literary references to illustrate his points much as the bible uses allegories and parables to present its teachings.

Bob really nailed it when he described the lack of a common bond among churchgoers. As with many in my circle of friends today, I felt no affinity with the religion my parents practiced, in spite of various efforts on their part to bring me around to their faith. Instead, I struggled for many years to find a place where I fit in, and the biker culture is now a huge part of my existence. It's a world where I discovered the true meaning of brotherhood and sisterhood, where I know that my true friends will tell me the truth, watch my back, or lend a hand when the chips are down—something I never experienced in my growing-up years nor in much of my so-called adulthood.

As part of my life journey, I spent 30 years in the corporate world—that's what my family did, so I followed suit—and was quite successful at it, winning awards and drawing a huge salary. But I never felt authentic. It never felt real. I was challenged to find my own authenticity, which has turned out to be writing and photography; recording an accurate telling of the motorcycle culture, as it were. I don't make nearly as much money as I once did, but it feels like I'm living my own life, in my own skin, for the first time.

Throughout the book, I saw Bob struggling with the same questions of faith, acceptance, freedom and honesty, and he poses a challenge to readers to pattern their lives on these principles. Look up FTW and you'll find scores of other meanings for this initialism.

The Internet-age description for FTW, For The Win, fits right into the premise of *I Just Wanna Ride*. To paraphrase a passage from the book, "They just wanna ride. They just wanna follow Jesus; FTW [For The Win]!" Forever Two Wheels is also quite popular in biker jargon, but my favorite is the now-arcane expression Free as The Wind. The author's libertarian leanings will absolutely strike a chord with those of you who, just like Bob does, interpret the biblical meaning of freedom to be "live and let live." FTW.

Marjorie Kleiman a.k.a. Shadow
Editor, Thunder Press North
Founding editor, American Iron Retailer
Freelance writer and photographer for many motorcycle publications

My relationship with Bob Kopp and exposure to this book began when I received his biker survey out of the blue and unsolicited. After much thought, I responded with this e-mail sent on May 26, 2009:

Dear Dr. Kopp,

This morning, to my surprise, I received an e-mail from a sender I didn't recognize and the e-mail had your survey attached.

I am a 1%er, as citizens – that's what we call everyone who isn't, including motorcyclists, and who aren't involved with a club like mine – call us.

We are not only a societal sub-culture, but a sub- culture within the biker community. We are often shunned or avoided or both.

Contrary to the reputation that my "type" has been saddled with, we are not a bunch of criminals, drug abusers, hell-raisers, etc. That reputation was probably deserved 30-40 years ago.

Today, most of us have families that we love and take care of. We go to work every day. We obey the laws that are fair and just. Granted, every "outlaw" club has a few bad elements and their behavior is not condoned. What causes us to all be painted with the same brush is due to the fact that we love our brothers dearly and are there for those individuals who screw up, right or wrong... and believe me when they are wrong, we let them know it! We can be very firm with those we love. We want them to be well.

I was fascinated with your survey and your research. However, I couldn't figure out where to begin filling it out because the questions are, in my opinion, geared toward the biker who jumps on his Harley on the weekends, attempts to "dress up" like us, and then return to their real life on Monday morning.

We, the 1%ers, are a complex group with a lot of nuances. It's interesting to us that the "weekend warriors" are parrots of each other trying to imitate what they think we are about. They do this with their attire, attitude, speech, and actions... often to a degree that is very funny to us.

The individuals in our clubs are just that – individuals. This is very important to us.

Weekend warriors do have a role in our world. They have become so prolific in number that they deflect a lot of attention from us... which is good. They have made it very hard for society and authorities to differentiate them from us.

Perhaps "Christians" are a lot like us. I've always contended that anyone can be a Christian for two hours a week, walk out the church door after worship, and go back to habits that are not Christ-like.

I have some Christian friends who truly live like Biblical Christians. They have my undying respect.

I've been asked by the weekend guys why someone would want to be in a club like mine. Usually, I'll size up the person asking and, most times, walk away. When I do sense the person asking is sincere and non-judgmental, I will try to explain the brotherhood, commitment, love, and respect we have for each other. This comes from the very long process one has to go through to patch out (become a full patch member). Interestingly, those other bikers think that once you've earned your patch, the work is done and you coast. Actually, you work harder. You are always conscious of the example you are setting for new or younger members, the work it takes sometimes to love and support a brother who has screwed up, to take every penny you have to help a club member who has fallen on hard times, and to conduct yourself in a manner that will not bring any disrespect to the patch or the club.

Wondering why the e-mail?

I feel your effort to explore our culture as metaphor and use it to challenge the church is fascinating and very interesting to me... and I thought that maybe a few thoughts put down from a 1%er might help a little.

Respectfully, Dave, Freewheelers MC

So it began!

A short while later, we met in person and what I found sitting across from me in the Mexican restaurant was, the best I could discern, an "authentic" (as Bob would say).

I decided this guy was worth checking out.

I attended the first summary sermon that he preached on the content that follows; and I am glad that it has become a book.

In my world, it is important to ascertain if someone is the real deal or just full of shit.

Attending subsequent services as he preached summaries of what will follow – the following is much rougher and real than what even he could ever get away with on Sundays – I quickly realized Dr. Kopp understands the "biker culture" every bit as well as he understands "Christians" in the church today.

Using the biker culture as a metaphor for challenging the church has resulted in this honest, witty, intelligent book written by an *authentic* biker and *authentic* follower of Jesus.

Bikers and church people alike will be challenged and encouraged by what has been written between these covers.

This book deserves respect.

Dave Moneysmith
Freewheelers MC
Sergeant at Arms

When Dr. Bob told me that he was writing a book that would probably offend people, my first reaction was, "Tell me more!"

He did.

I am hooked on what follows.

When we first talked about this book, I didn't expect someone of Dr. Kopp's character and credentials to *want to* offend anyone.

But as he caught my undivided attention, like the following pages will do to you, I began to pick up on some of the parallels in the biker community and church that provoked his probe and now report.

Actually, his life and mine have the kind of parallels that he writes about.

I love motorcycling and I sell Harley-Davidson motorcycles (He won't ride anything else for reasons that are very clear in the book!).

When we first met, he confessed not being a conventional pastor.

I said, "You wouldn't be talking to me if you were!"

I had to like him; because so many folks consider our sport and life to be on the dark side of proper society. While he knows our culture has a dark side, he also knows there's a bright side. *And he doesn't cover up for either in our culture or the church!*

So, yes, this book will offend people.

He exposes posers in both cultures.

He encourages the best from both cultures: charity, vitality, patriotism, freedom, and, well, *read the book!*

He's tough but tender.

He asks questions and has strong opinions but isn't judgmental.

In a very natural and easy to read way, Dr. Kopp uncovers the basics of humanity and describes the similarities, differences, challenges, and opportunities that have nothing to do with outward appearances, vices, or vehicles.

He just wants to ride.

He wants you to join him.

I say read this book and you just may end up riding to freedom.

Dr. Rus Howard
Pastor, Teacher, and Conference Leader

Bob Kopp is a mesmerizing writer.

Within the first five minutes of reading his work, you will love and loathe him. His honesty is refreshing and penetrating. He does not play favorites. He does not write to make you happy. He writes to challenge your thinking and your life.

Bikers will appreciate Bob's blunt-force-trauma honesty and genuineness.

Christians will appreciate his passionate love for Jesus.

Everyone will be moved by his insight – *moved to applaud him and moved to stone him!*

Bikers have a leg up on Christians. They are more genuine and they are more free.

Christians know about the genuine freedom they have in Jesus; even when they live constipated lives.

Bikers put everything on the line when they go for a ride.

Christians love to hedge their bets.

Bob Kopp is a biker and a Christian. He knows what it is like to FTW and *go for a ride.* He puts everything on the line without hedging his bets in this book.

Bikers develop intimacy with the world around them when they go for a ride. They smell the roses and the pig farms. They feel every change in temperature. They experience the glory of sunshine and fresh air; while enduring the challenges of rain, sleet, snow, and arrogant drivers who feel four wheels entitle them to recklessness.

Many Christians – *Well, let's be honest!* – have lost not only their way, but have also lost His way.

Bob Kopp will help bikers experience the genuineness of Jesus' love for them.

Bob Kopp will help Christians re-find His way out of the maze of their convoluted lives.

One final note before you saddle up and *go for a ride*.

Bring your dictionary!

Bob Kopp is a master of the English language. He does not *dumb down* his writing because you are unwilling to use the dictionary.

Wib Woodson
Former Finance Director
A Harley-Davidson Dealership

I'm not sure that a foreword is the right place for confessions, but since I'm writing on Bob Kopp's dime, I'm going to do it anyway.

I confess I am a frustrated Chicago Cubs fan. I know this statement is repetitive but I'm not being paid by the word... or at all for that matter.

I confess I have never been asked to write a foreword before; so what you read may be the product of enthusiasm, ignorance, or flattery.

And I confess I just don't get the whole biker culture!

I was not surprised that my friend wanted my help in writing this book, but given that my response to his purchase of another HD was something along the lines of, "I don't want to get a call from your wife telling me that they are picking up what's left of you with a shovel out on I-90," I have been wondering what I could contribute to his book about biker culture. I just don't get it.

I guess I understand something of the themes behind people who are both affectionate and offensive about riding. The concept of freedom is not foreign to me. I like freedom as much as William Wallace; so aptly played by Mel Gibson. The idea of being different from others is in my blood. I grew up in the 60s and 70s. The attraction of brotherhood is a passion for me. I would die for my closest friends.

The truth is, I believe, anyone can find liberty, uniqueness, and deep relationships without motorcycles, leather jackets, and bugs in your face. Those qualities are not external, after all, but internal, part of one's soul. I find freedom in driving my truck, uniqueness in the self-evident truth that there is no one else like me in all of human history, and brotherhood in the fact that I am eternally tied to a group of friends with whom I share life even beyond death. I find what bikers and everyone else is searching for in a common relationship with Jesus. In my opinion, everything else is personal style or fluff.

So I admit that while I get the motivations behind biker culture, I don't understand the need to take a risk of ending one's life by blowing a stop sign and ending up plastered on the side of a bus or sinking so much money into machines and clothing that could have been otherwise used to do something more constructive; like partnering with your friends and buying a small golf course. No, I just don't get it.

But Bob Kopp does!

What awaits you in the pages ahead, once you get past my confessional meanderings, shows a clear connection between the desires of our hearts and the behaviors of our hands. He writes as someone who not only understands the culture, but joyfully participates in it.

You are in for a treat and, I suspect, a surprise.

He'll be honest about himself and others; and if you'll be as honest, your life will become more and more what you dreamed it to be.

Enjoy... and learn!

Chuck Legvold
Senior Pastor

Preface

My youngest son Matthew (11 going on 17 *if you know what I mean*) and I went to Woodstock (Illinois) Harley-Davidson's 9th Annual Open House on March 21, 2009; featuring a live band, free food, storewide sale with some really great deals compared to typical HD (*aka* "High Dollar") prices, and other biker-friendly stuff.

Aside from my boy gobblin' down five burgers as I munched on a high-cholesterol brat or three, I was struck by his uncommon focus on what was happening around us; especially since he usually makes a poodle with fleas and ticks look sedate.

As soon as we climbed into our cage for the trip home, he started, "Dad, that was really cool! I've never seen so many different kinds of people in one place!"

Prompting him to utter what I already knew, he went on, "There were doctors and lawyers and auto workers and teachers and construction workers and a mayor and even a pastor-geezer or two like you. I even saw some old ladies who looked like Grandma French and Grandma Kopp."

Hesitating, he whispered, "There were also some really nasty looking guys and some sluts that I don't think mom wants me hanging around."

Finally, he concluded, "You know, dad, I guess everybody just came and got along so well because they all like to ride motorcycles."

His words hit me like three Stōks instead of the recommended limit of two a day on top of the boldest Chock full o' Nuts 24-councer available.

It was an apocalyptic moment; dredging up a deep often dark secret about the church that only now seemed appropriate to articulate for my son not to mention my 30+ years ordained clergy self.

Bikers – *as opposed to so many churchgoers* – have a bond that overcomes religious, political, color, class, and cultural distinctions that separate and segregate people from each other.

Just riding a motorcycle seems to generate an affection and affirmation among bikers that escapes much of today's church and society.

No wonder a "prospecting" friend has said to me on many occasions, "I'd rather be riding my motorcycle and thinking about God than sitting in church thinking about riding my motorcycle."

He also likes to say, "Only a biker knows why a dog sticks its head out of a car window."

Be that as it is despite the predictable protests of churchgoers, Matthew's observation troubled me.

It still does.

If Democrats and Republicans, liberals and conservatives, and people with two feet planted firmly in the air and people who hate to see anything happen for the first time along with the naughty and nice and just about every personality and ideological profile can enjoy each other's presence and more than co-exist like Arabs and Jews along the Taba Crossing at the Egypt/Israel border, why can't churchgoers do the same or, at least, present a reasonable facsimile?

It's because too many churchgoers don't have a common bond.

Too many churchgoers are so stressed out, separated, and segregated from each other over abortion, sex, money, politics, and whether Susan Boyle deserved to win over that ghetto dance team that not even Jesus bridges the distances between 'em.

It's tragic.

Instead of providing a beacon to a better way, truth, and life and safe haven for everybody regardless of who, what, where, or when, which is what its Founder was all about, the church has become host to "the most segregated hour of the week" (viz., Sundays during worship).

While most churches are horrified by homosexuality, they operate with such socioeconomic homogeneity that the heterogeneous intentions of their Founder are muted if not intentionally ignored; prompting a friend to write, "Yesterday, my 5 year old grandson made this statement: 'I hope Jesus comes back real soon, 'cause I'm kinda forgetting what heaven looks like.'"

People who really love Jesus by praying and laboring to love like Jesus look at the biker culture with envy; asking, "Why can't we get along as well as they can? Why does a motorcycle do more for unity among them than Jesus does for us?"

A big part of the answer is too many churchgoers aren't really Christians. They're to Jesus what RUBS (rich urban bikers) are to real bikers: posers, wannabes, couldas, shouldas, and wouldas; going from wild ones to mild ones like those churchgoing weekend warriors who whoop it up in the sanctuary and then live in the streets like any connection between them and Jesus is coincidental.

A slip at a wedding comes to mind; as the pastor began, "Nearly beloved... "

I know the following pages will piss off a lot of churchgoers; because I'm gonna use biker culture as a metaphor and challenge to the church.

I know some bikers aren't gonna be thrilled; because nobody's perfect and there are some bikers giving a lot of bikers as bad a name as some so-called Christians give to the real ones.

But as I like to say, don't blame Jesus for some Christians who need some Jesus in their lives; and don't blame real bikers for posers, RUBS, and the like.

By the way, that's how I came up with the title for this book.

I just wanna ride.

FTW.

I just wanna be authentic.

Real.

I'm reminded of famous conductor Reichel who was directing a practice of Handel's *Messiah*. The soprano soloist had just finished singing, "I know that my Redeemer liveth." Though technically on target, something was missing. Reichel challenged, "My daughter, you do not really know that your Redeemer liveth, do you?" Squirming a bit, she stuttered, "Why, yes, I, I do believe I do." "Then," Reichel thundered, "sing like you have the experience and joy and power of it!"

Bikers like to say, "People ask why we ride motorcycles. For those who have experienced the ride, no explanation is necessary. For those who have not really ridden, no explanation is possible."

A mentor put it this way, "My biggest struggle is not with people who don't believe in Jesus. I don't expect anything from them. My biggest struggle is with people who say they believe in Jesus but don't act like they believe in Jesus."

I'll paraphrase: "My biggest struggle is not with people who

aren't bikers. I don't expect them to understand. My biggest struggle is with people who say they are bikers but don't act like bikers."

Posers.

Frauds.

Liars.

Yeah, a lotta churchgoers and bikers are gonna hate me *in a Christian kinda way* for pulling their pants down in front of each other.

Jesus called it *salting;* doing what you gotta do to catch attention so you can save people from their damning proclivities.

Salt stings on an open sore but saves you from life-threatening infections.

Or something like that.

In short, I just wanna ride.

FTW.

Robert R. Kopp

Clarification

A friend from the South sent this story to me.

Two informally dressed women were talking during a long wait at the airport.

One was from California, arrogant, and married to a wealthy man.

The other was a well-mannered, elderly, Southern belle.

Talking about their children, the Californian started, "When my first was born, my husband built a beautiful mansion for me."

The belle commented, "Well, isn't that precious?"

The Californian continued, "When my second was born, my husband bought a BMW for me."

The belle commented, "Well, isn't that precious?"

The Californian continued, "When my third was born, my husband bought this big diamond necklace for me."

The belle commented, "Well, isn't that precious?"

The Californian asked the Southern belle, "What did your husband do for you when you had your first child?"

The belle answered, "He sent me to charm school."

Charm school?" the Californian blurted out, "Why did he send you to charm school?"

The belle answered, "Well, I learned how to say, 'Well, isn't that precious?' instead of saying, 'Who gives a shit?'"

Bikers and Christians have their own vocabularies.

While bikers will say what they mean and mean what they say, Christians will often play the game like the belle of that story.

Jesus said, “Let your yes be yes and your no be no.”

It doesn’t take too much discernment to figure out who’s more authentic.

Be that as it is, there are lots of biker books with big glossaries to help non-bikers interpret the tongues; and I’m only gonna define stuff if I feel like it or it’s really necessary.

Getting back to the title, FTW is one of those vulgar acrostics that’s easy to translate: “Fuck the World!”

Parenthetically, some churchgoers who only use such words when outta sight of other churchgoers like folks who sneak into their bathrooms to look at porn or wait until everybody’s asleep to get the really bad stuff on the net will pretend shock at the use of “shit” and “fuck” and other *common* words, phrases, recollections, descriptions, and the like in this book. They are myopically pretentious and pathetically phony; noting these same folks will focus on such minors while the world is going down the toilet quicker than poop through a goose.

Jesus had a rhetorical for them: “What’s that I see in your eye?”

Be that as it is, the “world” is a pejorative term for Christians who actually believe in Jesus enough to try to behave like they believe in Him; and the goal of their Christianity is to be “in but not of” it, overcome its seductions to behaviors antithetical to their confession as personified in Jesus and prescribed in the Bible, and give a shot at helping to transform it into something more to His liking by example, exhortation, and education.

So, in effect, authentic Christians are like authentic bikers.

They just wanna ride.

They just wanna follow Jesus; so FTW!

They don’t want the world to distract, detour, dissipate, or destroy their *real* experience of the ride.

The *authentics* share the passion of Martin Luther King, Jr.'s words on the night before his assassination (April 3, 1968):

> *Well, I don't know what will happen now. We've got some difficult days ahead. But it doesn't matter with me now. Because I've been to the mountaintop. And I don't mind. Like anybody, I would like to live a long life. Longevity has its place. But I'm not concerned about that now. I just want to do God's will. And He's allowed me to go up to the mountain. And I've looked over. And I've seen the promised land. I may not get there with you. But I want you to know tonight that we, as a people, will get to the promised land. And I'm happy, tonight. I'm not worried about anything. I'm not fearing any man. Mine eyes have seen the glory of the coming of the Lord.*

Anyone who has experienced the ride knows what King was talking about; while people who have not experienced the ride just scratch their heads.

But while authentics say FTW, they also have a passion for inviting everyone to ride.

An old Zen story from Garri Garripoli's *Tao of the Ride: Motorcycles and the Mechanics of the Soul* (1999) explains the compelling quest of authentics to invite, welcome, and include:

> *... a great master... dies suddenly. His closest disciple, also a greatly honored master, sits next to the body for two days and cries and cries. This really frustrates*

> *the monks of the temple as one of the edicts of Zen Buddhism is to practice detachment and to understand the illusory nature of all things. Finally, when the monks could take no more of this crying from their great master, they sent the eldest to confront the situation. The elder monk asked... how could he cry so if death was just an illusion. The master looked up with his bloodshot, teary eyes and said, "This is the saddest illusion I have ever experienced."*

But while authentics want everyone to ride, they have enough experience to know some will choose otherwise; and as we will note later, some of those who choose not to ride transfer their envious, devious, and intentionally destructive pathologies to those who do ride.

Authentics understand the theme of Robert M. Pirsig's *Zen and the Art of Motorcycle Maintenance* (1974): "The real cycle you're working on is a cycle called 'yourself.'"

Or as I recall a reviewer's comment on Hunter S. Thompson's *Fear and Loathing in Las Vegas: A Savage Journey to the Heart of the American Dream* (1971), "...a report of an actual experience which was largely fantasy or an actual fantasy which is disguised as report."

Yet, again, authentics have a *beruf* (call) to invite, welcome, and include; recalling Cain's question to God about Abel that God did not bother answering because the answer *is* so obvious to authentics: "Am I my brother's keeper?"

I have a friend who personifies the paradox of inviting, welcoming, and including everyone while saying FTW to those who choose otherwise.

He rides a Fat Boy with ape hangers and loud pipes that would make Captain America proud; but while dressing like an outlaw with representative patches all over his worn leathers, he has one patch hidden under his back collar that betrays his authenticity: “I Am My Brother’s Keeper!”

That explains the ubiquitous hand wave.

That’s why authentics feel “safe” in shops/churches “run” by authentics.

That’s why authentics will stop to “save” people on the roadside and not expect a response, regard, or reward.

That’s why authentics incarnate the greatest proof of authenticity that separates them from the posers as summarized by Jesus: “Love God by loving like God.”

That’s why this book is about biker culture as metaphor and challenge to the church.

I just wanna ride.

FTW.

Robert R. Kopp

Biker Culture as Metaphor and Challenge to the Church

Matthew's review of the biker rally mentioned in the preface sent me back in time.

I grew up in the backyard of the Pagans - a motorcycle club that remains among the dominant four outlaw "organizations" in America with the Banditos, Hells Angels, and Outlaws – during the late 60s; and though their roots can be traced back to Maryland, Pennsylvania seemed like the keystone of their growing empire from Parkesburg in the Southeast to Wilkes-Barre/Scranton in the Northeast. Though they've been expanding across the country and around the world since then, each of the dominant four had their traditional territories: Banditos mainly in Texas and throughout the Southwest, Hells Angels with their biggest chapters in California complemented by a scattering of others throughout the country, Outlaws in the Midwest, and Pagans in the East.

All of 'em, *naturally,* had challengers; but they were the biggest and baddest of the outlaw biker clubs.

I think Pennsylvania had more bars, brothels, and bikers per capita than any other state back then; and though I snuck into a bar or two before becoming legal, brothels weren't necessary for the Woodstock generation. Love and sex or even sex without love were free in the '60s and '70s; and, come to think of it, that may be the lasting contribution of my generation to American culture.

Because I was a lifeguard in the Poconos and gettin' enough trim without the trek to Max Yasgur's farm in upstate New York, I didn't go to Woodstock in August 1969; though I made up for missin' that one by makin' it to/at lots of other pop festivals and concerts.

That was August.

Easy Rider was released on June 26, 1969; and I saw it about a dozen times.

I've been a biker ever since; and if you come to my study, you will spot the soundtrack about two feet from my desk and maybe hear it playing in my Bose if positive providence is with you.

Confessionally, I listen to "my/our" music a lot; and though it brings back a lot of good memories of those early biking and boinking rides in Pennsylvania, I've gotta be careful with music as a husband, father, and pastor. Music aligns the head, heart, gut, and gonads.

When I listen to Grace Slick, Joni Mitchell, that chick singing with Meatloaf about *Paradise by the Dashboard Light,* or even Sarah Brightman and especially Alanis Morissette, I ain't thinkin' too much about Jesus.

Be that as it was, I'll never forget Wyatt (Peter Fonda's "Captain America"), Billy (Dennis Hopper's hopped-up simpleton), and George Hanson (the alcoholic ACLU lawyer portrayed by Jack Nicholson in his first major film role); especially that scene about freedom that continues to haunt America that I'll get to later.

Wyatt became the archetype of the poet-biker in search of America's soul.

Billy was the drugged-out-live-for-today-because-he-had-no-clue-about-anything-except-a-physical/emotional-rarely-intellectual-erection.

George was close but confused or so plastered most of the time that he was too confused to stay close.

Some metaphors bridge the gaps between generations.

Regardless, biking got into my blood from the first scene with Wyatt tossing the watch as Steppenwolf sang "Born to Be Wild."

Though Woody Stevens played by John Travolta popularized the cry to ride in *Wild Hogs* (2007) – "I just wanna ride, man!" – newbies like me were pickin' up the chant and takin' to those Pennsylvania roads with gusto on our HDs, Triumphs, and metrics/rice/burning/imports.

I hopped on my first bike, roared down Sans Souci Highway from Nanticoke to Wilkes-Barre moments after forking over $25 for it with my brown flying-fringed leather jacket from Juarez that Ollie got for me when he crossed over from El Paso during his freshman year at UTEP, and screamed along with John Kay.

It was a Honda 50.

Gotta start somewhere; and I've been turning on the fuel supply valve, switching on the ignition, shifting the transmission into neutral, turning the cut-off switch to run, pullin' the choke, hittin' the starter button, and gettin' ready to shift into first for the next ride for 40+ years.

Jay Leno and I have something in common: "The first bike I ever got was a Honda 350 back in 1971... I remember getting on the freeway, thinking, 'This is fun!'"

There are lots of us: "The baby boomers were the driving force behind the new interest in motorcycling... These were the same people who had bought all those little Hondas in the 1960s, who had terrorized the highways on thundering Kawasakis in the 1970s, and who had spent the 1980s raising kids... Now their kids were grown up, and they once again found themselves... " (*The Complete Idiot's Guide to Motorcycles,* 2008).

Whether it's a biker emerging from hibernation after years of vocational and familial necessities or a biker who has weathered the years and stayed up more than down, they've got a bond that is undeniable.

Again, the ubiquitous hand wave is a clue.

Bikers passing in opposite directions will give a fist pump or drop the left hand to signal a bond not requiring familiarity.

The bike alone bridges all gaps; rendering individualities subordinate to the nobler value of unity not demanding homogeneity.

Bikers who have never nor will ever see each other again wave in a profoundly spiritual expression of affection and affirmation.

Then there are those churches that have got to designate greeters in some kinda ecclesiastical "Welcome Wagon" because "members" don't have enough common sense or faithfulness to the invitational, welcoming, and including intentions of their Founder to extend more than the backhand of Christian fellowship.

My favorite contradiction is the need to take time from worship to "pass the peace" or get out of the pews and acknowledge each other's existence and take a nano-second or two to feign friendliness; as if *or because* the Founder cannot expect those who love Him to love like Him and pass peace before and after the one holy hour of the week.

It's like the time that I followed a car with a "Honk If You Love Jesus" bumper sticker. I honked. The driver gave the finger to me.

I'll never forget the couple who came to me for counseling. The wife said, "He's never around. It's either work or playing with the boys." He said, "Well, she says she wants me around; but whenever I'm around, all she does is bitch and moan. Why would I want to be around someone who says she wants me around but treats me like shit when I'm around?"

That guy understands a common biker slogan: "Bro's before bitches."

Before hyper-feminists get off on such biker lingo, it has nothing to do with gender. It's about authenticity; which is more about spirit than gender.

Churches need to confess more than cite Mark Twain's conclusion about too many churchgoers: "The church is always trying to get other people to reform; it might not be a bad idea to reform itself a little by way of example."

Churches need to go with Matthew to a biker rally.

Churches need to ask why bikers refer to motorcycle club meetings as *church*.

Churches need to ask why bikers are so obsessed with being considered *righteous*.

The answer is bikers have a community (church) and commitment to that community (righteousness) that is rarely mirrored in too many of today's churches.

I'm not saying all bikers are authentic.

Posers mount mules as well as park in pews.

They slither in among authentics and often give 'em a bad name; and while we're not gonna blame the authentics for the inauthentics, we've got to acknowledge 'em.

For example, there are really bad bikers; or as Matthew said after the biker rally in Woodstock, "There were also some really nasty looking guys and some sluts that I don't think mom wants me hanging around."

Just riding a bike doesn't make a biker; just as much as just sitting in a church doesn't make a Christian.

God as well as authentics know that.

When we get to the chapter on "Clubs," we'll mention some of the intrigues, idiosyncrasies, facts, and fictions about 1%ers who have been stereotyped as outlaws but come in as many varieties for good, bad, and ugly as Christians come in denominations; or as John Hall said so well, "I'm not saying that all one-percenters are saints. But neither are all cops, priests, or politicians" (*Riding on the Edge,* 2008).

I think of asking my friend Ted who rode home to Jesus not that long ago to estimate the percentage of mainline clergy who actually believe in Jesus as attested in the Bible. He said, “Maybe 40%.”

Authentics are 100%ers.

They are *real*ly committed to the best of who they claim to be.

It’s like the resurrected Peter Fonda’s character Damien Blade said to some bikers who had lost their way in *Wild Hogs,* “Why do you think I don’t wear the colors, Jack? Why do you think I ride alone? ‘Cause you don’t know about it anymore. I think you oughta get back on your bikes and go out and ride the highway until you remember what riding’s all about.”

The Hells Angels come to mind.

I’ve met good ones and bad ones.

Yeah, they’re all tough; like a local 81er – 81 is a metonym as the 8th letter of the alphabet is “H” and the first is “A” which refers to the obvious - said, “If you treat us well, we’ll treat you better. If you treat us bad, we’ll treat you worse.”

Then there was the biker funeral a few years ago in Loves Park, Illinois. After the service and interment at the cemetery, I asked a few 81ers who showed up, “What would you guys have done if somebody had cut in on the biker and car procession from the church to the cemetery?” An HA about my age said, “We’d peel off, pop their tires, and get back in the procession.” Then I asked if they wanted to go back to the church for the reception and meal. They all begged off; except for one who said, “Hey, man, I’d go for sure; but my granddaughter has this recital at her grade school in a few hours.” I said, “I won’t tell, dude.” He said, “Thanks, man.”

There’s a lot of truth in their name itself. It’s Hells Angels rather than Hell’s Angels; because “there is more than one Hell, it just depends on who and where you are” (Jay Dobyns, *No Angel,* 2009).

Authentics want to drive out darkness by being light; like the Christophers say, "Light a candle rather than curse the darkness."

Authentics in biker culture and church understand Mother Teresa's prayer:

Dear Jesus,

Help us to spread Your fragrance everywhere we go.
Flood our souls with Your spirit and life.
Penetrate and possess our whole being so utterly
    that our lives may only be a radiance
    of Yours.
Shine through us
    and be so in us
    that every soul we come in contact with
    may feel Your presence in our soul.
Let them look up and see no longer us
    but only Jesus.
Stay with us
    and then we shall begin to shine
    as You shine,
    so to shine as to be light to others.
The light, O Jesus, will be all from You.
None of it will be ours.
It will be You shining on others through us.
Let us thus praise You in the way You love best
    by shining on those around us.
Let us preach You without preaching
    not by words, but by our example

by the catching force
the sympathetic influence of what we do
the evident fullness of the love our hearts
bear to You.
Amen.

Simply, as all authentics know, in her concise and compelling yet surprisingly comprehensive words, "Our vocation is to belong to Jesus."

When I sent out a survey to help me probe biker culture as metaphor and challenge to the church (see the appendix), I asked, "What is a 1%er?"

Here's a sampling of the responses:

My son Daniel: "The bad ass ones who give the wrong picture of bikers to people."

HD salesman: "Member of a motorcycle gang whose life revolves around it."

Pastor: "A nut job, by choice or by accident."

Pastor: "See Webster's under, Obama, Barack."

Pastor: "A very rare breed."

1%er: "We are a sub-culture within the biker community. Contrary to the reputation, we are not a bunch of criminals, drug abusers, hell-raisers, etc... For us, it's all about being non-judgmental and brotherhood, commitment, love, and respect."

Teacher: "Felons who have complete disregard for societal rules and behavior."

Auto Worker: "We live by our own rules; not by society's."

Retired: "They think they're bad to the bone; until real bullets hit and then they cry and scream like babies just like the other 99%."

Pastor: "A biker who makes it to old age."

CEO: "The baddest of the bad who do not represent the other 99%."

Now here are my two favorites from pastors:

"It's what most people give on Sundays."
"Christians who pretend to tithe."

While I respect the authenticity of self-proclaimed 1%ers, authentics are all about being 100%ers; which, just to peek down the road, is what I think authentic 1%ers are really all about no matter what the American Motorcyclist Association said after the events of Hollister, California back on July 4, 1947 which "inspired" Hollywood's version of what happened in *The Wild One* (1951) starring Marlon Brando: the rogues who rode over Hollister's bike rally were "the one percent of the American motorcycle riding public that is criminal."

While the AMA has never recanted its conclusion about 1%ers being "the 'rough' element of the motorcycling public... [as opposed to]... most motorcyclists... [99% who are]... good, clean, God-fearing Americans with jobs and families" (Dave Nichols, *One Percenter: The Legend of the Outlaw Biker,* 2007), I'm more in consonance with John Hall's conclusion:

> *... the AMA published a pamphlet proclaiming that 99 percent of the motorcycle riders in America were hard-working, God-fearing, tax-paying, flag-waving, church-going, milk-sipping, cookie-eating, law-abiding citizens, and that the average American had nothing to fear from these people when they rode past on Sunday afternoons. It was the criminal element... the shit-kicking, beer-guzzling, gang-banging, ass-stomping, rock 'n' roll playing, hell-raising heathens and devil-worshiping hooligans who belonged to "outlaw clubs," which were not affiliated with the AMA.*

Hall continued,

> Outlaw clubs, *the AMA again claimed, accounted for less than 1 percent of the people who rode motorcycles but accounted for 99 percent of all the crime, mayhem, and bad publicity associated with motorcycles... But... I saw plenty of AMA motorcyclists raising hell... Criminals are crooks who manipulate the system to get rich. Outlaws simply don't give a shit.*

It's the cry of the authentics: "I just wanna ride. FTW."

Or to twist a phrase to be in consonance with my conclusion from a comment on December 10, 2007 that was posted in response to "Understanding the 1% Rule" on Church of the Customer Blog, "You gotta be 100% committed to being known as the outlaw 1% who don't follow or conform to mainstream society."

Yes, this book looks to biker culture as metaphor and challenge to the church; not because it's pure and perfect and that much better than the church or any other culture *but because it provides a very powerful paradigm – as diverse as it can be at times – of what is good, bad, and ugly in the church.*

I'm not suggesting I know everything about biker culture or the church; but, as Robert M. Pirsig suggested, "Sometimes just the act of writing down the problems straightens out your head as to what they really are... The road has become so dark I have to turn on my headlight now to follow it through these mists and rain."

With so many bastardizations of authenticity, I'm just tryin' to find the way, truth, and life; or as biker's often say, "It's the journey not the destination."

Or going back to the resurrected Peter Fonda's character Damien Blade in *Wild Hogs* in an unmistakable not so subtle reference to the watch toss in *Easy Rider,* "Ride hard or stay home. Oh, and guys, lose the watches."

That's authenticity.

Be real and stop posing.

That's biker culture as metaphor and challenge to the church.

Robert R. Kopp

Definitions

Solomon, the 3rd King of Israel and David's son who fulfilled his father's wish by building the Temple in Jerusalem, was renowned for his wisdom and wealth; and he also opened the door to false gods on God's turf and was so horny that he stockpiled wives that proves even the wealthiest and wisest of us are certifiably human about lots of stuff.

How many periods and pauses can one man endure?

Although this book isn't about gender politics or exposing the folly of idolatries – *Oh, I guess there are more than inferences here and there* – Solomon probably could have *prophet*ed from an exchange during a caring session with a troubled guy who said to me, "The bad news is my wife is going through menopause. The good news is it will only last for a few decades or 'til death do us part.'"

Be that as it is, a lot of Solomon's wisdom is just plain old common sense; unless, of course, you've got so little of it that it's elevated to a higher status when someone like Solomon comes along to tell you about it so you don't make too many *un*wise miscues.

Here's my favorite: "Without a vision, people perish."

Without dreams, people dry up, drop out, and die.

It's axiomatic.

We get better or worse but never stay the same.

I think of the church lady who scolded me when I got back on my bike, "Aren't you a little old to ride a motorcycle?"

I snorted back, "I'm not dead yet."

I feel so sorry for people who have stopped trying new things, risking, probing, exploring, and so on.

I feel so sorry for people who say, "I never change."

That's like saying, "I never live."

I prefer some wisdom shared with me from a graduating high school senior who signed my yearbook when I was in 8th grade: "May you live as long as you want to and want to as long as you live!"

Yes, God does not change.

He is always sovereign, Savior in Jesus, and encouraging and enabling as Holy Spirit.

But we better be those wineskins that can stretch and expand with the new blessings of opportunity and adventure that He offers so consistently or we'll be as boring, dreadful, and death-filled as, well, so many folks just going through the motions.

A conversation with my mom about my dad comes to mind.

My dad is addicted to buying golf clubs; because, like all authentics, he's always looking for ways to improve.

My mom said, "Your father is over 80 years old and he's still filling up the house and your sister's basement - where he thinks he can hide them from me – with all of those damn golf clubs of his."

I said, "Well, mom, when dad stops buying golf clubs, let me know; so I can clear my calendar and fly in for his memorial service."

It's all about having some idea of who you are; because who you think you are goes a long way in contributing to your zest for living and peace of heart, mind, and soul.

I'll never forget hearing Edie Brickell sing back in 1986:

I'm not aware of too many things.
I know what I know if you know what I mean.

What I am is what I am.
Are you what you are or what?

It provoked an apocalyptic moment.

I was still that boy wonder who had climbed to the top of the ecclesiastical ladder of success only to discover I was leaning against the wrong building.

I was not filled with joy and had a hole in my heart as big as the open borders of the USA.

Listening to that song over and over and over again, I realized I had no idea of who I was; evoking another recollection about the guy who says to a friend, "I don't know who I am or where I'm going." His friend responds, "Don't worry! Most folks are going through the same thing."

That may be tragically true; but it doesn't have to be so!

Jesus said, "I have come that you may life; and have it abundantly!"

Putting that together, I agreed with Walt Whitman ("Song of the Open Road", *Leaves of Grass,* 1855):

... I take to the open road... From this hour, freedom!
... I ordain myself loos'd of limits and imaginary
lines... divesting myself of the holds that would
hold me.

Sure, I've made lots of mistakes since then; and I'm gonna make more!

Indeed, the only folks who I've ever met who don't make mistakes are dead already.

They are dead men/women walking.

If you haven't figured it out yet, that's a big part of what this book is trying to help you avoid.

This book is all about being who He made you to be and riding; because only when you are who you are can you feel the wind beneath your wings.

Matthew and I went to another biker rally on June 13, 2009: "The Great American Biker Jam" hosted by Kegel Harley-Davidson of Rockford, Illinois.

While the food wasn't free this time, which limited intake, we got into the vendors, bike shows, bands, and, as expected, undeniable bond despite the unmistakable diversity of bikers.

Confessionally, I went because I bought a raffle ticket; and really wanted to win the 2009 Road King because I've promised to hand over my 2003 Dyna Wide Glide to Matthew when he's "ready" *if you know what I mean.*

I know some fundies who think that's gambling.

Maybe it is.

I'm not sure.

Didn't the apostles cast lots to replace Judas?

O.K., that's a rationalization.

Well, I never claimed to be God's other son like lots of holy people who act like it until they're "caught" in their less-than-divinity *if you know what I mean.*

It's like the church lady who barked at her pastor for cutting the grass on Sunday. He said, "Jesus fed the poor on the Sabbath." She said, "Two wrongs don't make a right."

I knew the odds were against me; but as my dad says, "The odds are really bad if you don't buy a ticket."

I'll buy more; and if you're a pastor who never took a vow of poverty but serve a congregation that imposes it upon you, you know why.

We also spent a lot of time with the local chapter of the Christian Motorcyclists Association.

Matthew got into the free stuff for kids and I got into the free books, tracts, and conversation.

I like CMA.

They know it takes more than loud pipes to save lives.

They know who they are:

> *The main purpose of CMA is to share the gospel of Jesus Christ with motorcyclists... The patch we wear on our clothes identifies us as a group of men and women who like to ride motorcycles, but we ride them with a purpose in mind. We put the the words "Riding for The Son" around our name to show that we have found a reason to live and ride. That reason is knowing Jesus Christ as our personal Savior and we desire to share His message of love and forgiveness with others.*

The first part of that quote comes from *Hope for the Highway* (1999), which is a New Testament with "biker" notes, and the second part is from a tract called *Everything You Ever Wanted to Know About a Motorcyclist... But Were Afraid to Ask* (1992).

After expressing its *self*-awareness, CMA asks in the tract, "What is the message you tell others?"

It's the same as Edie's declarative followed by her interrogative.

As laudably *self*-aware as CMA has been since its genesis over two decades ago, they may try a little too hard to be "with it" and may cross over into *posing* and turning more off than on to Jesus; especially when it comes to all of their patches that make the most decorated Boy Scouts look like pikers or Cheryl Crow following Dolly Parton to the beach.

Authentics smell inauthenticity as readily as capitalists smell socialists in Washington, D.C.

Posers are easy to pick out of the line-up.

Certainly, as Arthur Veno pointed out in *The Brotherhoods* (2002), "There's no such thing as your typical biker. Everyone is different, with each having their own reasons for getting into bikes."

That's true.

Individuality is part of the ride's freedom.

As part of *The Mammoth Book of Bikers* (2007), Ross Fuglsang observed, a motorcycle "becomes the 'very icon of wildness.'" Then he quotes Willie G. Davidson: "The bike conveys a mechanical forcefulness – it's not totally tamed."

Or as one HD salesman responded when I said I didn't consider myself to be a typical undertaker-looking-tail-between-the-legs-pussy-of-a-pastor: "If you weren't a little off, we wouldn't be talking."

Despite the individualities, there's a lot of conforming in biker culture.

Bikers have their vestments, vernacular, and sacred music; betraying *uniform*ity amid diversity that Vincent Colnett and George Wethern described as "incredibly individualistic yet as tight as blood brothers" in *A Wayward Angel* (1978).

More than less, bikers talk and dress alike; or as Jay Dobyns, the guy who knows all about posing, mocked the Hell Angels as representative of biker culture in general: "...they're nonconformists, but they all look the same."

As undeniable and unmistakable *is* the tie that binds biker to biker, making it nearly impossible to distinguish societal segregations of education, vocation, and the like when you're with a bunch of 'em, that *same*ness contradicts the swaggering to vitriolic claims to uniqueness.

More than less, bikers have been dressing like Marlon Brando's *The Wild One* since 1953; though the quality of merchandise has improved since HD's entrepreneurial genius began including apparel and accessories.

"What're you rebelling against, Johnny?" Mildred asked Marlon's main man in Hollywood's version of the biker fun and fiasco that occurred during that early biker rally in Hollister, California in the first few days of July 1947. Johnny answered, "Whaddya got?"

Surely, biker culture joins *Easy Rider*'s Billy in a ceremonial finger to the controlling pathologies of church and society; but gives the hand wave, fist pump, and high five to remarkably conforming vestments, vernacular, and sacred music.

CMA doesn't really have to try as hard as they're trying to fit into biker culture.

All they have to do is buy a boatload of HD stuff; which, I see/swear/surmise/suspect includes pants, chaps, denims, jackets, vests, rain gear, T-shirts, tank tops, shoes, socks, sunglasses, goggles, beanies, belts, bandannas, boots, gloves, woolies, hoodies, halters, hats, headbands, helmets, lip balm, jewelry for *every* part of the body, money clips, wallets, watches (Move over, Captain America!), a whole line of pet products, condoms, and tampons *sporting* HD in big, bold, and bonding letters.

O.K., I exercised a little hyperbole; but you've got the picture.

How individualistic is it for everybody to wear the same stuff from the same company?

Even biker culture cannot escape the herd mentality.

Psst.

I think the quality of HD's biker paraphernalia as well as mules is unparalleled; even if they're HD (again, *aka* "High Dollar").

Confessing jingoism, primarily because of unfair and inequitable labor and trade practices, I'm with Jay Barbieri (*Biker Handbook,* (2007):

> *Harleys are as bulletproof as any bike out there and have some of the most advanced technology available... Harleys are too expensive... Too bad. Owning an original part of history is priceless... the least you could do is buy an American-made motorcycle and be part of the culture that defined freedom on the open road.*

Despite messing up their name in the title with his apostrophe, Hunter S. Thompson understood the bias of the largest part of American biker culture: "The little bikes are fun, handy, and relatively safe... while the big ones are two-wheeled bombs, and the outlaws who ride them would rather walk than be seen on a Honda, Yamaha or Suzuki" (*Hell's Angels,* 1966).

The biggest part of biker culture is as biased as churches that either think God stopped inspiring new music after 1952 or didn't start inspiring it until 1985. You won't hear any Captain and Tennille, Tony Orlando and Dawn, or Olivia Newton-John singing "I Honestly Love You" or "Have You Ever Been Mellow?" around bikers; though you might hear Olivia singing "You're the One That I Want" with John Travolta from that last scene of *Grease. Sooooo hot!* Biker music includes overdoses of Jimi, Janis, Cream, Doors, ZZ Top, Mountain, Cocker, Dead, Airplane, The Who, Lynyrd Skynyrd, Led Zeppelin, Willie, SRV, Seger,

Springsteen, Stones, Steppenwolf, AC/DC, Aerosmith, and other hard-drivin', ass-kickin', boot-slappin', back-seat-humpin', and beer-guzzlin' goodies that never seem to grow old to 'em.

How Elton John ever got to Milwaukee in 2003 remains a mystery.

Then there are the tattoos and piercings.

Yeah, tattoos are individualistic – depicting something "special" to the inked like a symbol, picture, name, or significant date – but if everybody on a bike is inked, how unfettered and free is that?

Respect for Leviticus 19:28 and other body-as-holy-temple texts are subordinated to the self-willed need to "express" feelings, beliefs, or the results of a bad trip or binge of any sexual or substance-abused nature; or as the fellow with enough tattoos to pose as a Mother's Day floral display for Wal-Mart said when I asked why, "Because I can. Nobody can tell me what to do with my body."

Personally, I don't get it.

I don't like pain of any kind, can't imagine how tattoo artists would have handled the changing names of whoever was the current best babe in my life, and shudder to think how I'd pick out a booger from my nose if I had one of those rings in it.

*More*theless, I guess it is kinda individualistic; or as a church member suggested as the title for this book: *Don't Be Fooled by the Outside!*

Fact is I've seen lots of funky lookin' folks who love a lot more like Jesus than those who look the part but are only posing.

If God cares more about the heart of the matter than what's ornamenting the temple, it should be good enough for us.

It's not; but it should be!

It should be because people are like snowflakes: different yet beautiful *in their own way*.

Here's how the Psalmist put it: "I have been remarkably and wonderfully made." He prefaced that with praise to the Creator: "It was You who created me."

God Himself pressed the point through Jeremiah: "I chose you... I formed you... I set you apart before you were born."

As long as somebody's loving God by loving like God, what makes us think we've got the right to suppress their funkiness?

That's why I have so little patience anymore for people who exalt so-called traditional over contemporary sacred music and vice versa. If God inspired all of it, who the hell do people think they are in dissing one over the other?

If God made people to be bald and others to be shaggy-headed, what right does anyone have to pass judgment on their hairstyles?

You know what I mean.

Some folks act as if the Bible – it's the same thing for bikers whose bibles are motorcycle owners' manuals and the latest epistle from Sonny Barger or just released and never-seen-before sayings of the late Indian Larry, – isn't bigger than their favorite parts.

Of course, *ought* and *is* don't always coincide in *any* culture.

Isn't that what Wyatt and Billy found out at the end of *Easy Rider?*

You could see it coming when George Hanson warned Wyatt and Billy when they first got together:

> *Well, you boys don't look like you're from this part of the country. You're lucky I'm*

> *here to see that you don't get into anything... Well, they got this here, see, uh, scissor-happy "Beautify America" thing goin' on around here. They're tryin' to make everybody look like Yul...*

Wyatt and Billy were gunned down because they didn't fit into an image and would not pose or bend forward for any attempted imposition.

Pirsig's Phaedrus ran the same risk: "He didn't give a damn who liked or didn't like him. He was single-mindedly pursuing a truth he felt as of staggering importance... The world had no idea of what he was trying to do and it was trying to kill him for his trouble."

Jesus knew all about that; and anyone who tries to love Him by loving like Him will not avoid His cross even if it's a crowning celebration *in the end.*

Using Christian authenticity as a model for others despite the inevitable risks, Pirsig wrote,

> *... A good sermon can put the parishioners in a right frame of mind for the coming week. Sunday school will help the children grow up right... The minister... also knows that his primary goals are not to serve the community. His primary goal is always to serve God. Normally there's no conflict...*

Pirsig, sadly, is wrong in that last phrase because there's always a conflict when conforming images are expected; as there's always an Edie, Walt, Wyatt, or Billy around to extend that ceremonial finger.

Authentics know the risk – they've seen/experienced it over and over and over again – but the reward of real life and real liberty are worth it to 'em.

CMA caught the mood in a little tract called *He Would Have Ridden A Motorcycle* (1992):

> *He was a lot like you and me. The government didn't like Him. The church thought He was weird. His friends were few. What friends He had, denied Him. He was persecuted by hypocrites. He hung around people like you and me, not the goody-two-shoes Pharisees.*
>
> *Yes, if Jesus were on this earth in the flesh, He would be next to you on His motorcycle telling You He loved you... enough to die for you.*

Though I've admired him for many things over the years, I was really turned off by the bigoted witness of Pat Robertson back in 1991 that sounded so unlike Jesus:

> *You say you're supposed to be nice to the Episcopalians and the Presbyterians and the Methodists and this, that and the other thing. Nonsense. I don't have to be nice to the spirit of the Antichrist. I can love the people who hold false opinions, but I don't have to be nice to them.*

Where in the hell did he come up with that bullshit?

If "God so loved the world," who does he think he is?

Here's what I've learned over the years and repeated so often for folks who have been bruised, beaten down and up, battered, and butchered by bigots of conformity:

God does not want to tear us down, pick us apart, burn bridges, fracture families, degrade, denigrate, devastate, or destroy us.

That's the work of Satan.

God builds bridges, relationships, friendships, families, and reconciles, heals, helps, includes, enables, elevates, enlightens, and encourages.

Satan says, "You're no good. You're bad. You're useless. You don't belong."

God says, "Come to Me."

God invites and includes.

God loves.

Authentics are like that; bonded by mutual affirmation, affection, and allegiance that overcome the diversities.

Spiritually, authentics have to pray and work on it.

The apostle is right: "All have sinned and fall short."

When a friend heard I was writing this book, he asked for the theme. I said, "Bikers are as screwed up as churchgoers but more confessional about it and have a culture evoking important questions for churchgoers." He wrote back, "We all fall short of the glory of God; but when bikers fall, they get hurt a lot more."

My friend likes metaphors too.

I know I'm wrong about lots of things; and if I'm shown the error of my ways and witness by comparison to the highest authority of Biblical Christianity, I'll confess and repent.

I'm still travelin', dude!

I don't expect to arrive 'cause I believe folks who think they've arrived haven't begun.

Or something like that.

I just wanna ride.

FTW.

Getting back to patches, I've got two on my vest. I've got "100% Saved" just above one with those three vulgar-for-the-ignorant and righteous-for-the-authentic letters: FTW; and when I find a big "100%er" patch, I'm gonna *cover my back* with it.

I'm praying to be a 100%er when it comes to the best of biker and church culture.

A big part of being an authentic or 100%er is accepting who *you* are by His design and accepting who *they* are by His design and not feeling better or worse or inclined to impose *your* image on *them*.

Putting it another way, being created in His image means conforming to anyone else's imposed image is disobedient to His determination.

Or something like that.

While everybody's got an opinion on who we are or should or could be like everybody's got a you-know-what, the only thing that matters is who we are by His design.

But when you're ridin' down the road, it doesn't hurt to know what's comin' or around the corner.

It's what the Motorcycle Safety Foundation understands as SEE: (1) Search the factors before you that present risk; (2) Evaluate the factors for potential risk; and (3) Execute a strategy to minimize risk and maximize a margin of safety against risk.

Or as a biker might say, "Watch out for bastards in cages who don't give a fuck about you and'll cut you off quicker than a bitch on the rag."

Bikers have an image for good, bad, and ugly as I've known since mounting my first mule; and I was reminded that the passions about those who ride often equal the passion to ride in this sampling of responses from the survey as related to the first three questions: (1) "What is a biker?"; (2) "Why are you a biker?"; and (3) "If you're not a biker, what do you think of bikers?"

Supervisor: "A biker lives on the edge. Freedom is a big deal."

Funeral Director: "It gives me an outlet when I can enjoy the awesome scenery of this country. I think most bikers are so patriotic because they actually see how great this country is."

Spiritual Punching Bag (*aka* Pastor): "A biker is a 'freebird' as LS sang. It's someone with the guts to say 'to hell' with conventional wisdom. I'm so envious as a non-biker because I want their freedom."

Pastor: "Bikers are wild and crazy."

Project Manager: "Bikers need freedom like everybody else with the difference being they grab it around the throat!"

Retired Construction Worker: "Bikers come in good and bad. They're just like church people and everybody else in that regard."

Teacher: "Bikers are free-minded and free-thinking and refuse to conform or blindly follow anybody."

Pastor: "Like church denominations, there are good ones and bad ones."

Pastor: "...an individual with an incessant need to explore the number of bugs that can be smashed into a face, the number of cars that he can avoid colliding into, whether one's brain is really damaged in a crash, and such other things that fly in the face of being normal."

Pastor: "I like some and dislike others – depends on their attitudes on and off their bikes. Overall, I think bikers are on the downhill side of crazy because they put their lives at risk whenever they ride."

HD salesman: "It's about escaping everyday issues for a while."

CEO: "Bikers have a passion for riding; understanding its inherent dangers and riding nonetheless. They enjoy 'oneness' with nature."

Teacher: "I am not a biker... but I wish I were. I'm jealous of their freedom."

Homemaker: "...big time partyers and risktakers."

Homemaker: "I find the majority of them to be scary. It must have something to do with the whole bad boy thing."

Dispute Manager: "I think they are looking for moments of freedom."

Pastor: "I don't really think of bikers that much; except when I see one of those jackasses on a crotch rocket who is speeding to a place to crash."

Teacher: "Bikers come in all sizes and shapes and dispositions just like everybody else. Most of them are very nice, normal people and then there are a few that give the sport a bad name. Isn't that the way with all people – pastors included?"

Retired COO: "...anyone who enjoys the pure pleasure of riding an open road with the wind blowing through their hair... They are the most egalitarian, trustworthy, and honest network of individuals I know of."

Public Relations Manager: "...a person who disregards the insane danger of his vehicle for the thrill of getting bugs in his teeth. They seem to have an adolescent craving for adrenaline... seem wholly self-centered for the joy of engaging in unsafe locomotion."

Contract Administrator: "...a person who rides these days is just about anyone who grabs a bike and goes – minus the crotch rocket brats who are still trying to impress."

Teacher: "I got a bike because it was cheaper than a shrink. Besides, shrinks are even crazier than us!"

Caretaker: "Bikers operate on their own frequency. I'm envious. They're so free and I'm so stuck in boring neutral which is a synonym for normal."

Pastor: "Bikers are more interesting than most people. That's because they're always exploring and expanding their horizons."

Retired: "My husband had a bike. I got one after he died. Such a sense of freedom! So relaxing! Ever notice how children wave to bikers? That must be a clue."

Retired: "O.K., they're free. I want to be free. Just don't ask me to ride. Maybe that's why I'm not free."

I'll let you know my occupation when I have one: "Bikers are naïve. That's better than being normal."

Teacher: "Bikers are dangerous to themselves. Sometimes annoying. Rebels. The ride seems like such an unnecessary risk."

Unemployed: "I'm not a biker; but I love riding on the back of a bike with the wind in my hair, seeing everything, and wrapping my arms around the driver."

Hair Stylist: “There’s something so sexual about it all. I get hot just thinking about bikers. They’re so free. They seem to have their shit together and only shit on people who shit on them.”

Pastor: “I don’t have many bikers in my church because they’d never put up with the crap that I do. They’re so sure of themselves that they can’t take being around church weenies.”

Semi-retired: “O.K., I’m a biker; but most of us haven’t fully matured yet and need to live on the edge. Yet, that feeling of the ride! That feeling of freedom when out on the open road with the wind in your face and the odors... all of it accentuated by the symphonic sound of my Harley.”

I don’t work: “A biker is a burly, hairy, bear of a man who is a little crazy with a renegade spirit but loyal to other bikers and the object of every woman’s fantasy.”

HD salesman: “I am a biker because it gets me away from all those stressed-out types in your churches. BTW, I agree with you on lean machines. Though I sell ‘em, I’m with you about not creating a garbage wagon with audio, CB, GPS, and all of the other shit that I ride to avoid. BTW, that’s why I leave the bitch at home.”

Succinctly, there's a lot of diversity amid the *uniform*ity paralleling the biker bond.

Yet, there is still that thread of authenticity connecting all authentics.

Pirsig was right about motorcycle mechanics – a righteousness that all authentics share: "The difference between a good mechanic and a bad one... is precisely this ability to *select* the good facts from the bad ones on the basis of quality. He has to *care!*"

Sam Jones wrote for *Thunder Press* (May 2009):

> *... riding motorcycles, being a biker, a real motorcyclist... has a lot more to do with it than just hanging out with 20,000 of your closest friends, trailering in your custom Harley and wearing a vest festooned with patches and pins. You want to know what it meant to be a biker... One thing... the mileage you put on your bike. Chrome and fancy paint meant nothing. Only the mileage stood for anything. Everything else was just posing.*

The only way to experience the "strong calm sanity" (a favorite phrase of Oswald Chambers to distinguish posers in the church from those who are really intimate with Jesus) that separates authentics from posers is to be who you are according to His design.

As Mr. Rogers used to say, "Just you!"

I take my neighborhood friend one more step: "God loves you just the way you are but too much to leave you just the way you are."

You'll never be authentic with *strong calm sanity* until you sing "Savior, Like a Shepherd Lead Us" and not worry if time permits.

You'll never be authentic until you change your *horizontal* perspective of caring how others define you to a *vertical* perspective of only caring how He has designed you.

That's at the core of zestful living with unceasing excitement and adventure.

It's like the scene in *The Wild One* in which Kathie asks Johnny, "Well, what d'ya do? I mean, do you just ride around or do you go on some sort of a picnic or something?" Johnny scoffs yet heralds at the same time: "A picnic? Man, you are too square. I'm... I... I'll have to straighten you out. Now, listen, you don't go any one special place. That's cornball style. You just go."

It's the urge of authentics as articulated by the apostle: "Seek the things above, where He is! Don't set your sights so low!"

Don't let anyone but the Highest define who you are!

Spend all of the time that's necessary to discover His design!

FTW.

Ride!

Robert R. Kopp

Addictions

The Dead Poets Society (1989) is one of my favorite movies; except for the end when another authentic dies, commits suicide in this instance, because he will not return to caged life after riding to freedom.

It's about an English teacher named John Keating who returns to his stodgy old alma mater named Welton Academy – the students call it "Hellton" which reminds me of so many churchgoing children who can relate because there's nothing more soul-draining than people chained to the ordinary and so addicted to boredom (Ask a child why she/he doesn't like "church" and they'll blurt, "It's so boring!" That's why I open almost every homiletics class at any graduate level this way: "If you aren't excited about Jesus, quit now! You ain't gonna get anyone else *into* Him if you ain't! Spice things up! Take some risks! Ride to the edge! Because there's nothing worse than preachers who bore 'em to death! And, friends, that's another metaphor!) – and challenges students to live extraordinarily.

"The Dead Poets Society," he reveals with eyes aglow, "was a society dedicated to sucking the marrow out of life. That phrase is by Thoreau and was invoked at every meeting."

He continues, "A small group of us would meet at the old cave, and we would take turns reading Shelley, Thoreau, Whitman, our own verse – and in the enchantment of the moment let it work its magic on us."

"You mean," a student asks, "it was a bunch of guys sitting around and reading poetry?"

"Believe me," Keating answers with increasing energy, "we didn't simply read... We let it drip from our tongues like honey. Women swooned, spirits soared... gods were created, gentlemen."

He begins the first class with these words:

Gather ye rosebuds while ye may,
Old time is still a flying:
And this same flower that smiles today,
Tomorrow will be dying.

"The Latin term for that sentiment," Keating explains, "is *Carpe diem*... Seize the day!"

Then he says, "One day, hard as it is to believe, each and every one of us is going to stop breathing, turn cold, and die."

Pointing to pictures of their predecessors at *Hellton,* he urges,

> *Look at the faces of the boys who attended this school 60 or 70 years ago. Don't be timid; go look at them... They're not that different from any of you, are they? Hope in their eyes, just like yours. They believe themselves destined for wonderful things, just like many of you... Did not most of them not wait until it was too late before making their lives into one iota of what they were capable? In chasing the almighty deity of success, did they not squander their boyhood dreams? Most of those gentlemen are fertilizing daffodils now! However, if you get very close, boys, you can hear them whisper... "Carpe diem... Seize the day... Make your lives extraordinary!"*

One day in class, Mr. Keating (played, by the way, by Robin Williams) inspires Todd Anderson (played by Ethan Hawke) to ride to freedom – to seize his extraordinary potential; and a powerful poet emerges from the shy, silent, and cowering boy. As the scene closes, Mr. Keating walks to Todd's side and whispers into his ear, "Don't you forget this."

That's riding with freedom *once you get it*.

That's authenticity; or as a plumber responded to why he is a biker in the survey: "I enjoy the raw-ness."

Sadly, too many folks stay parked in pews and never mount mules to life, liberty, and the pursuit of happiness.

Sadly, too many agree and submit rather than overcome and ride with the truth and challenge of an old Shaker tune: "It's hard to dance with the devil on your back."

Sadly, Bob Seger's lament becomes a theme song for folks who are stuck in neutral: "So you're a little bit older and a lot less bolder than you used to be." Recalling another of the Detroit rocker's songs, too many folks are more like silly putty than solid rocks (viz., *Like a Rock)*.

Sadly, there's so much bitchin' and moanin' with John Cougar, "O yeah, life goes on long after the thrill of livin' is gone."

People seem so addicted to what brings 'em down rather than lifts 'em to life, liberty, and happiness.

That's why Mr. Keating often taught while standing on his desk; for when explaining why, he roused more than reported, "I stand upon my desk to remind myself that we must constantly look at things in a different way."

I am convinced Jesus was talking about the existential as well as eternal when He promised, "Behold, I make all things new!"

Sadly, so many folks seem so addicted to life with such limited possibilities that they miss the opportunities right in front of 'em.

That's why authentics on bikes will often talk about the life, liberty, and happiness of feeling the wind beat against 'em, smelling all of the smells including the stinky ones, the exhilaration of dramatic temperature changes at so many turns and ups and downs, and seeing so much that is so abridged, blurred, and blotted out when confined to those vehicular *and other psychosociospiritual* cages.

While I'm not an expert on addictions – though over three decades as a pastor and almost 60 years of occasionally addictive behaviors are kinda instructive – I've come to differentiate the positive from the pejorative ones; or as Mr. Keating put it, "Sucking the marrow out of life doesn't mean choking on the bone."

I've come to understand the difference between pejorative addictions that inhibit life, liberty, and happiness and positive addictions that enable life, liberty, and happiness.

Concisely, most folks who know more about it than I do define an addiction as any activity, substance, object, person, or anything else that becomes the most important focus, feeling, and fact of existence to an excessive emotional, intellectual, spiritual, and physical dependency or inability to "go on" without it.

It's the difference between "I just *wanna*" to "I just *gotta*."

It's the difference between "I just *wanna* shop, run, play golf, ride, eat, fuck, buy lottery tickets, go to Vegas, or *whatever...* " and "I just *gotta* shop, run, play golf, ride, eat, fuck, buy lottery tickets, go to Vegas, or *whatever...* "

I know trouble's brewin' when somebody says, "I need my fix of... "

When somebody says they "cannot live" without someone or something, a tragedy awaits its time.

The plumber/biker's contemplation of a harrowing ride is illustrative: "There is a huge rock along the stagecoach trail heading toward Galena, Illinois that reads 'Jesus Saves.' So as you're riding and reading at the same time, you almost miss the fact that there is a sharp left turn. Now if 'Jesus Saves,' He might have said, 'Caution! Sharp left turn ahead!'"

A pejorative addiction becomes so compulsively self-*un*controlling that everything and everybody else rides bitch to the addiction; more often than not manifesting itself in deceit, detachment, depression, self-denial, rationalization, and so many psychosociospiritual maladies that jobs are lost, families are ruined, and lives are paralyzed in a downward spiral of captivity to the addiction at the expense of everything and everybody else with disastrous to deadly inevitabilities.

Or something like that.

The problem is bad things taste good.

That's why they're so tempting.

I've never been tempted to eat a steak covered with maggots; but if the steak is rare, fresh off the grill, and covered with garlic butter, I could be distracted from my next cholesterol check-up.

I've never been tempted to make out with a woman whose mouth is covered with oozing sores; but if a woman takes care of herself and is remotely as hot as Sophia Loren *at any age* and smellin' better than Ivory Soap and strokin' her hair while lookin' at me in one of those dead giveaways of kindlin', I could find myself rationalizing with the beast in me, "Thou shalt not commit adultery *unless it's just unavoidable."*

Parenthetically, I'm with Walt Whitman:

Women sit or move to and fro, some old, some young,

The young are beautiful – but the old are more

beautiful than the young.

I've heard people who should know better say sex is the greatest temptation for a young man, money for an older man, and power for a mature man; but my experience – personally and pastorally – is any of the three can pop up at any time like an erection in 8th grade when the close-to-retirement old bag has to share time with the few-years-out-of-high-school-herself student teacher...

Be that as it is while standing on top of my desk, the pejoratively addicted often don't entertain the consequences of their behaviors; requiring other bonds to intervene to help heal.

Sexual addictions are so tragically illustrative of the challenge to even the best of bonds.

I think of an associate pastor who loved women of all sizes, shapes, and styles; and knew, as an older elder warned me years ago with *eventual* success, "The easiest way to slip off their panties is to pray with them."

So many women are so hungry for attention and conversation that just makin' 'em smile and sharing a cup of coffee with 'em will get 'em between the sheets.

That's a heeding not a hint!

God knows guys like me in any caring profession haven't had any problems attracting and bedding women; because it's our business to listen like good humor men who are trained to pose interest if not provide counsel.

I used to think it was *me*; until I heard somebody say that women attracted to Henry Kissinger prove the virgin birth of Jesus.

It's true.

If women will fuck guys like him, Marilyn Manson, grungy rockers, gangsta rappahs, and even effeminate pastors, it's not that flattering when one of 'em wants to fuck you.

By the way, if you're offended by the "F" word here, I use it because the experience is as shallow and profane as folks whose vocabulary is so limited that they use it as a noun, verb, adjective, and so on.

So I told my associate who was warming up to one woman who was especially hot for him, "Listen, man, I agree she's really attractive and I wouldn't mind a day or two on a deserted island with her or at least a room in the city; but she's like so many of them out there. You'll have great sex with her; but after she's hooked you, she'll want to control you and both families will be destroyed in the process."

That's the problem with pejorative addictions.

They end up controlling your gut, heart, head, and loins; and hurting more than the primary *players*.

Transparently, I've always been a sucker for affirmation and affection.

I like sex.

I like to make out with long sloppy kisses, cuddle, fondle, lick, suck, and fuck *for hours*.

It's an orgasmic oasis in a world and church of cold showers.

I'm limited by the experience of the consequences for dippin' in the past.

While my experiences aren't as extensive as antagonists fantasize, I've had enough to know that pejorative addictions could have destroyed me as well as too many others if left unchecked, uncontrolled, and, ultimately, unconverted.

My last adultery over a decade ago almost did that.

This is not the context to labor the circumstances; but a few recollections are instructive.

She wanted to make out with long sloppy kisses, cuddle, fondle, lick, suck, and fuck *for hours*. She had millions ($); and wanted to share her gut, heart, head, loins, and everything else with me. She told me to abandon my call and family and join her somewhere/*anywhere* for a lifetime of sloppy kisses, cuddling, fondling, licking, sucking, and fucking.

It sounded good to me.

Psst.

Still does.

Again, I'm with Whitman: "I am he that aches with amorous love."

But then came the apocalyptic moments catalyzed by the kinda bonds that should be in the church but are more often a part of biker culture.

A biker buddy took me aside and said, "Bob, she's gonna eat you up and spit you out before you know what hit you. She's swept you away and will sweep you out just like she's done to every other guy in her life."

Then came the God moment. When I talked about my responsibilities as a father and husband and that I still believed my wife would be as hot for me as I've always been for her, she said, "Don't worry about it! You will be able to see your children on weekends and every now and then."

It was like God had slapped me in the face like Cher slapped Cage in *Moonstruck* to snap me out of it.

That was over a decade ago; and while I'm still tempted every now and then, especially when her needs and my needs ain't matchin' up, the consequences are so severe that the temporal *fix* ain't worth it.

I've come to realize temptations are bad things that taste so good so temporarily; going down so smoothly while causing such gut, heart, head, and even physical indigestions that they just ain't worth it.

Personally and pastorally, I don't underestimate the temptations; especially, again, when her needs and his needs aren't matchin' up.

Specifically, folks who know a lot more about this than I do say a man's essential needs are sexual fulfillment, recreational companionship, an attractive spouse, domestic support, admiration, affection, allegiance, and respect. A woman's essential needs are affection, allegiance, conversation, honesty, vulnerability, transparency, financial support, and family commitment.

More or less.

My favorite poet, John David Burton, expressed the *need* so well in *Naked in the Street* (1985): "I need someone to touch who will touch me and let me know that I am alive... When I see her I touch her and by her I am touched. Thus we let each other know we are alive."

Simply, women and men have needs; and if those needs are not being met by her/his spouse, those needs will be met *by someone else sooner or later.*

Crudely, if she/he ain't gettin' it at home, she/he's gonna get it with or without him/her; or as Stephen Stills sang, "...and if you can't be with the one you love, honey, love the one you're with... "

Loudon Wainright III sang about mutually unmet needs:

Whatever happened to you
Whatever happened to us
We missed the proverbial boat
The plane and train and the bus
Push came to shove and we fell out of love
We tore each other apart
Love is grand but I can't understand

Why you broke my proverbial heart

We used to be in love but now we are in hate
You used to say I came too early
But it was you who came too late
Boy meets girl and they give it a whirl
And the very next thing you know
She thinks he's nuts and he hates her guts
Then the bad blood starts to flow

Well it sounds like sour grapes
And that's just what it is
Gonna get me a subscription to Argosy
And I'll get you a subscription to Ms

That's a whole lotta crap
About a tender trap
What it is is a suicide snare
All I wanna do is to forget you
And our lousy love affair

While knowing there are three sides to every story – her side, his side, and the truth – I warn both of 'em that if one of 'em is holdin' out and not puttin' out that it's gonna catch up with 'em sooner or later and usually sooner than later.

An old cartoon comes to mind. Archie says, "There's nothing worse than warm cola." Jughead corrects his friend, "Yes, there is. No cola."

While there seems to be as much infidelity in the church and most cultures as biker culture, the phallic nature of motorcycles seems to turn up the heat of women for men who ride 'em.

Anyone who has mounted a mule knows there's no shortage of women who want to be mounted by bikers; or as Sonny Barger, the proverbial founder of Hells Angels asserted on several occasions, "A lot of 'respected' women are secretly drawn to wilder, more macho guys while the so-called sensitive guy stands there with his dick in his hand. It's just human nature for a lot of chicks; that's what turns them on."

Bikers know how easy it is to score with a "biker chick" or "fender bunny" or... There are lots of really degrading synonyms out there.

At a biker rally that I attended without Matthew, I was getting the bottom of those two aforementioned patches sewn on – the woman who was doing the sewing had a sticker on her machine that blared "My Second Favorite Toy is a Dick" – when a woman rubbed against me from behind and made it clear that she wanted to know if I was up for sowing *despite her husband or partner or whatever being at the other counter under the same tent;* proving Peter F. Hummel's point: "We all followed the sage advice of old Samuel Johnson... about the pursuit of females of easy virtue, which goes something like: 'The position is ridiculous, the pleasure is fleeting, and the expense is damnable!'" (*Motorcycles, Christians, and Heathens,* 2005).

Some folks don't sense or see the consequences; *operating* with Bob Seger's "Night Moves": "We weren't in love, oh no, far from it... I used her, she used me... But neither one cared... "

"These were country girls," John Hall wrote of the *attraction*, "who grew up in the valleys attending church on Sunday, but during the rest of the week they listened to songs like 'He's a Rebel' and 'The Leader of the Pack'... they dreamed about... riding through the cool night air with their arms wrapped tightly around a bearded barbarian... "

Hall went on,

> *It was weird. If we saw these same women on the street the rest of the week, we would not recognize them and they might be mortified if we did. But on Monday night they wore their hair differently, they wore more make-up, and they had special outfits – boots, tight jeans, trashy blouses, and leather jackets – that they saved for when they came down looking for cheap thrills.*

Amy Keyishian, a freelance writer from New York who has contributed to many of America's most successful reads, confirms Hall's suspicion that "most Americans are rednecks and outlaws at heart, but are afraid to admit it":

> *We've all heard that women want a guy who's tall, dark and handsome. But maybe it's time to update that to "tall, dark and handsome – and on a Harley." Because it seems that since the days of the flicks The Wild One and Easy Rider, a guy on a bike has held a special kind of bad-boy appeal. In fact, in a recent Match.com survey, "motorcycle" was the second most popular term that women used when searching through online profiles.*

[... Why?...]

> *"Motorcycles are still perceived as rebellious, tough, and strong" ... Like tattoos, motorcycles are often the hidden fun-factor...*
>
> *There's no doubt about it: a motorcycle signifies a little extra ingredient in a guy – a little extra testosterone in a world of sensitive men. Hey, sensitive heterosexuals are great, but some women still like a little cave with their man. "A man on a bike exudes independence, self-reliance, and fearlessness... He has nothing but leather between him and certain harm – clearly, he freely embraces risks and has a lust for life." Yes, that rebel vibe can work its magic.*
>
> *... women swoon [Hello, Mr. Keating!]...*
>
> *... Of course, some women don't dig the biker thing at all... To which we say: "Doll, you're born to be mild."*

My friend with the "I Am My Brother's Keeper!" patch hidden under his back collar said over breakfast during a break in a ride, "It's good to be happy and single. It's better to be happy and married. It's bad to be unhappy and single. It's the worst of all to be unhappy and married."

That's why so many women and men are on the prowl these days; and there are lots of women and men out there in biker culture, the church, and just about all other cultures who are eager to jump into the breach.

While there's always some *mama* around to satisfy unmet needs whenever, wherever, and just about with whomever, *old ladies* are a protected class of women in biker culture. You don't mess with a biker's *old lady* and escape biker justice which is swift and convincing.

Translation: *Mess with another biker's old lady and you're gonna get the shit kicked out of you by the biker and his buddies even if you're one of his biker buddies!*

The biker bond includes protecting the exclusive rights of the biker to his *old lady;* which, more than less, is a kinda synonym for wife.

Indeed, biker culture protects that relationship a lot more than the church protects the exclusive privileges of marriage between one man and one woman.

Yeah, I know bikers can still fuck *mamas* if their *old ladies* are pausin' or periodically not into it; but that still doesn't change the inviolate nature of the biker having an *old lady* who is not be treated like a *mama.*

Or something like that.

God knows *as well as everybody else* that the church has become a sexual free-for-all with no room to be condescendingly judgmental about any other culture's sexual proclivities.

Be that as it is, regardless of the addiction to *whatever,* not even the biker bond or that occasionally authentic bond among churchgoers can overcome addictions.

That's when the greatest bond of all must be acknowledged, addressed, and assimilated; using the discovery of Alcoholics Anonymous – first few steps that seem to parallel the Decalogue as setting the tone and enabling the others; noting AA's use of the steps to overcome alcohol is transferable to overcoming other addictions - as among the most effective paradigms of overcoming pejorative addictions (from *The Twelve Steps of Alcoholics Anonymous):*

> *We admitted we were powerless... that our lives had become unmanageable... Came to believe that a Power greater than ourselves*

> *could restore us to sanity... Made a decision to turn our will and our lives over the care of God...*

Essentially, AA's paradigm is remarkably reminiscent of the recipe for renewing a relationship with God – again, like AA's paradigm, it is transferable to all relationships – that is outlined in Revelation 2:1-7: "*Remember* then from what you have fallen; *repent,* and do the works you did at first."

Remember everything that made you so passionately in love.

Repent and do them all over again.

Here's how AA outlines the plan as excerpted from *Twenty-Four Hours a Day* (1954):

> *What makes AA work? The first thing is to have a revulsion against myself and my way of living. Then I must admit I was helpless... The next thing is to honestly want to quit the old life. Then I must surrender my life to a Higher Power, put... my problem in His hands...*

That's confession; remembering His intentions for your life, liberty, and happiness and how you've been detoured by succumbing to so much less than His best for you.

You cannot fix what you will not face; meaning you cannot overcome an addiction that you will not acknowledge.

Then AA talks about the repentance – turning from the pejorative addiction of who and what take you away from His best for you and turning to a positive addiction to His best for you – that requires the time for intimacy with

Him; an intimacy that always bears the fruit of His best for you:

> *It doesn't do much good to come to meetings only once in a while and sit around, hoping to get something out of the program... The new life can't be built in a day. We have to take the program slowly, a little at a time. Our subconscious minds have to be reeducated. We have to learn to think differently.*

While AA's positive addiction is to overcome the pejorative addiction to alcohol, the "program" is like being born all over again to authenticity or God's best design through the confession (admission) and repentance (action) that always leads to restoration (overcoming the pejorative addiction and replacing it with the positive addiction):

> *There are two important things we have to do if we want to get sober and stay sober. First, having admitted that we're helpless... , we have to turn our... [addiction]... over to God and trust Him to take care of it for us. This means asking Him every morning for the strength to stay... [clean]... and thanking Him every night... Second, having given our... problem... to God, we must cooperate with Him by doing something about it ourselves.*

In other words, the best way to overcome a pejorative addiction is by replacing it with a positive addiction.

It's hard to admit that some addictions that we think are positive are really negative; for addictions are always pejorative when *just gotta* replaces *just wanna* and injures others which always injures us as we ignore His always best designs for us.

Getting on my bike and getting away from it all as a retreat to restore energies and enthusiasm for returning to the world with the goal of making it a better place for all – I like how Garripoli calls it a "legitimate monastery" to restore Chambers' "strong calm sanity" and, as Mother Teresa counseled, "...free our minds from all that is not Jesus... " – is such a positive addiction; yet it becomes so pejorative when my bike becomes more important than loving Jesus by loving like Him and nothing more than the chromed phallus for self-serving masturbations.

Biker culture at its best has that bond that challenges cultures like the church to the extraordinary; and the *extra*ordinary sees beyond the ordinary/natural/navel-gazing selfishness to a persistent passion – let's say *addiction* – to something better for all as best personified in the greatest lover of all time: Jesus.

He came to leave no one behind.

He came to love with only one condition; that people who say they love Him would practice not pose His unconditional favor for everyone regardless of who, what, where, or when without the need or expectation for response, regard, or reward.

He came to lead a ride to wholeness, happiness, joy, and security.

He came to show us how to suck the marrow out of life; but not choke on the bone.

He came to break our chains and liberate us from the cages of anyone and anything that would keep us in neutral.

He came, as the apostle wrote, so we may be transformed into the extraordinary instead of conforming to a world of such boring control and suppression of Godly spirit: “Do not conform to this world, but be transformed by the renewing of your mind, so that you may discern what is good, pleasing, and God’s design.”

So given the options, Jesus is the best addiction.

That’s why He urged, “Don’t love anyone or anything more than Me!”

He was saying, “Ride with Me and you’ll be safe, secure, and saved now and *then.*”

That’s why I just wanna ride with Him and for Him.

FTW.

Mandatory Ride - Sturgis, South Dakota

Getting it/Him! - Sturgis, South Dakota

Easy Ridin' in the Badlands

Originals - Sturgis, South Dakota

Basics

Whenever Ruth called to meet with me, I knew she'd be bearing *bad news*.

Most churchgoers are like her.

Guys like me spend most of our time with people who bitch and moan about everyone and everything; and suck the marrow out of our lives.

Or, at least, they try.

It's a vocational hazard.

The only way to keep our heads above their cesspools of condescending speck-inspections via pseudo-spiritual superiority is increasing intimacy with Jesus that bears the fruit of more than tarrying with Him: love, joy, peace, patience, kindness, goodness, faithfulness, gentleness, humility, and self-control.

And God knows it takes all of those supernaturally enabled qualities triggered by increasing intimacy with Him to deal with people who bring everything but heaven into your life.

Yeah, I just wanna ride.

FTW.

But when you're getting paid by folks who feel entitled to dump all of their bullshit on ya...

Well, you know what I mean.

It's like the shrink who said during some graduate studies, "The problem people in your churches are usually constipated. That's why they dump on you."

People are more pissed off than ever these days; and they need scapegoats – objects to transfer all of their *pissed-off-ness* to take some of the load off 'em.

Having hung around those kinda folks for so long, I think things have gotten much worse since 9/11/01; and if you've already forgotten what happened then, it ain't gonna be any help tryin' to bring you up to speed 'cause you're already too far down the wrong road.

Anyone with any modicum of discernment knows the anxieties attached to that event coupled with an unabated global war led by religious nutballs (mostly Islamists), fainting economies, vocational insecurities, distrust in government, and all of the other stuff that inhibit life in the modern world from being a hot fudge sundae have caused the unraveling of personal and corporate *strong calm sanity*.

People are pissed off, freaked out, and looking for somebody to dump on to make 'em feel better about how awful they feel about all of the shit in their lives.

Even churchgoers who should know better are acting uncharacteristically these days; contradicting the peace, unity, and purity of intimacy with Him and transferring their pejorative pathologies to others to assuage/avoid personal pain.

Even people who say they love and trust Jesus are acting like any connection between them and Him is coincidental; coming unglued at the

slightest sense of insensitivity to their preoccupations and divorcing themselves from the body – church – when service above self, a hallmark of discipleship, loses out to rationalized infidelities masquerading as fidelities.

A friend who isn't a biker but caught in the same vocational nightmare as me, admitting he'd get out if he could like the 75% of all clergy who would quit today if they could ($), wrote about the problem at my request:

> *I think one of the reasons people are so crabby and out of sorts these days is that we have lost the equilibrium of our younger days.*

The answer to everything now is to do more, do it longer, do it harder, and do it better than anyone else.

In times of economic fear, especially after people worked so hard to get to the top of their economic potential, our only response seems to be to either work harder or give up and bitch about it.

It's my observation that people were less bitchy when I was growing up. Yes, there were the grumpy old codgers who didn't want you walking on their lawn and the crabby old ladies who thought that getting their morning paper after 6:00 a.m. was like getting their breakfast at noon, but most people were much more tolerant and tolerable – even the kids. Revered lawyers let us tear up their front yards playing football and mothers with eight kids of their own offered cookies and milk to neighborhood kids.

Why were people less crabby back then?

I think it is because we have fallen away from the way God has made us. We are made to live in cycles, and sometimes even in ruts or routines if you like. God made us this way and set up plans in His creation and His law to reflect it: seedtime and harvest, the seasons of nature, the Sabbath rest.

We have pushed ourselves into believing that we can overcome and improve God's way of living by doing more and working harder; when all we end up doing is making ourselves tired and miserable.

So what should we do?

Instead of making school years longer, thinking we can educate our kids by trying to cram more into them, let's make them shorter; returning to a real summer vacation that lasts from Memorial Day to Labor Day. Let's make evenings times of rest; rather than running off to one more meeting at the church or one more game at the fields. Let's make weekends a time for family labors, fun, service to the community, worship, and nothing else. Let's refuse to cram our calendars with one more game, meeting, obligation, errand, shopping trip, or political rally. Let's take our days off and our vacations, and really be off and vacated.

It we do so, there is more time to recover the equilibrium we have lost. We will save money on fuel, eating out, and all of those incidentals that we just have to stop and buy on the way to and from the next event. We will save personal energy that can be put in reserve for being patient with crabby people who won't choose to do so.

> *And along the way, maybe we'll save our families, our schools, our churches, our nation, and our sanity.*

Not bad for a non-biker!

Yeah, it's *all of the below*; or maybe those hyper-Calvinists are right and we're just all so totally depraved since the garden despite Jesus that the only sanctuary from it all is to take time off as my friend suggests and ride with the many authentics in biker culture and few who remain in the church.

FTW.

Getting back to Ruth, I knew she was coming because her perfume could knock over a bull at fifty paces.

She sat down with her hair looking like she used super glue to keep it so fashionably 50s, a pretty tight sweater for a tight broad that reminded me that even the tightest of broads can be cracked *if you know what I mean,* one of those SNL church lady smirks on her face as she started, "I hear there's going to be some juicy stuff at the board meeting tonight. Oh, goodie, goodie! I just love a good fight!"

I responded after posing a bit about her perfume and hair: "Please tell me how fights are redemptive. I may be wrong; but I don't remember Jesus saying anything about liking to fight. I need your help on that."

She had no answer.

They never do.

It's like the anonymous response to the survey's questions – anonymity is a clue as people who respond to anything/anyone anonymously are emotional terrorists who lack the courage of their convictions and like to operate *in the dark* – about biker identity (What is a biker?) and challenges to those who ride (What is the biggest threat to a biker's safety?). In letters rivaling HD's boldness on their apparel, the respondent (euphemism) wrote, "TWO WORDS: BODY PARTS!" regarding the former and "WHO CARES?" regarding the latter.

Isn't that special?

Yep.

People, for many reasons, are bitchy these days and there aren't many of us who can avoid being splattered by their spewings.

While churchgoers will fight about almost anything from carpet color to changing the worship times to using real wine or Welch's for the sacrament as if His kingdom rises or falls on that kinda bullshit, bikers don't like to fight unless they're drunk, someone's messin' with their old lady or old man, or one outlaw MC has violated another's turf.

Usually, bikers just wanna ride, talk about riding and stuff related to riding, and be left alone *even if they're at a rally with a whole bunch of other bikers.*

Bikers just don't bitch a lot while riding; which kinda confirms my friend's insights about equilibrium.

But if you want to start a fight with bikers, just say something like this: "Everyone who rides a motorcycle should be required by law to wear a helmet."

That'll start a war that would make the Outlaws and 81ers proud!

Though I started biking a long time ago in Pennsylvania when helmets were required by state law, I'd always take it off as soon as I crossed into a state that didn't require one; and now that I'm living in a state that doesn't require me to wear one, I don't for several practical, rebellious, and ideological reasons: (1) I feel more at-one with my surroundings without a helmet; (2) I am convinced an experienced rider is safer without one because peripheral vision is expanded along with increased awareness of the sights, sounds, and smells that are integral to increasing margins of safety; (3) I have an, uh, overriding aversion to anyone who isn't educated or experienced telling people who are educated or experienced how to do what they don't do; (4) I'm weary of the intellectual inconsistency of cultures, for example, that threaten the safety of the unborn but wanna make me wear a helmet for my safety; (5) Farmers are right: "Don't interfere with somethin' that ain't botherin' you none!"; (6) Actually, I wear one when riding through big cities just in case some smart ass thinks bikers are good targets for drivebys and from overpasses; and (7) I wanna give hope to people who hate me *in a Christian kinda way*.

Yeah, I've heard the statistics like "wearing a helmet improves your odds of surviving a crash by 37%."

The Motorcycle Safety Foundation, which I applaud with enthusiasm and without hardly any equivocation while encouraging everyone who wants to ride to take their superb courses before saddlin' up or as refreshers if you've been out of the saddle for a while or even to remind you of things that you may have forgotten or bad habits that you've picked up over time that threaten safety, is declarative about it:

> *Helmets work well in accomplishing their intended function to protect the head and brain from injury. Some myths about helmets are that they cause neck injury, block vision, or impair hearing. However, helmet effectiveness has been confirmed by research, not just in the laboratory, but by decades of actual crash analysis as well. So, be safe and always wear a helmet while riding.*

Most authentics aren't gonna argue about it.

They'll say, "Hey! If you want to wear one, be my guest; but don't try to make me wear one or I'll bust you up!"

People who don't really give a shit about me one way or another in the church will insist I wear one for my safety *but,* again, *they really don't give a shit about me which means they are more into control than care!*

Don't underestimate the control needs of people who will control whomever they can.

Just like churchgoers who fight over the aforementioned asinine stuff and so much more *which is irrelevant to ultimate realities but so relevant to their need to control others by imposing their asinine bullshit on others,* most of the angst around helmets is really people, overwhelmingly from the non-biker world, wanting to control somebody else's ride.

Hey, people want to be free to do their thing; and if it isn't hurting anyone else or infringing on somebody's else's freedom, why would anyone want to restrict their liberty?

Control.

Pirsig defined 'em: "Hundreds of itsy-bitsy rules for itsy-bitsy people."

A biker buddy from Virginia drew a parallel pour moi: "The first testicular guard 'cup' was used in hockey in 1874. The first helmet was used in 1974. It took 100 years for men to realize that the brain is also important."

Now if I have to explain that to you, there's no hope that you *can* understand the helmet conundrum.

Truth is wearing a helmet won't do very much for you if you're wiped out by an 18-wheeler or something like that; though your head may look pretty in the casket.

I like this exchange between Dudley, Doug, and Woody in *Wild Hogs*. While holding up his helmet, Dudley exclaims to Woody, "60% of motorcycle fatalities can be avoided by using the proper protective headwear." Doug blurts out, "What's that leather condom gonna protect you from? Snoopy? The Red Baron? Dating?"

If you're really concerned about safety, mandate motorcycle safety courses, mandate state bike inspections to make sure they're safe for the ride, and dress appropriately for the conditions.

In other words, some things are basic to the ride and some things aren't; and a lot of it depends on your personal comfort level juxtaposed to generally accepted margins of safety.

"If you're a biker," I asked in the survey, "what do you carry when you ride?" Essentially, I wanted to know what bikers consider *basic* to a safe and satisfying experience. The responses were revealing:

Plumber: "Tools, maps, water, notebook, rainsuit, cold weather gear, sun block, and a woman."

Project Manager: "Weapons, tools, and a rainsuit."

Sheet Metal Worker: "Smokes, water, money for gas and food, gear for all weather, clear glasses for night riding, and condoms."

Pastor: "Towel, tools, rain gear, extra sunglasses, money, and whatever's necessary for the circumstances of a particular trip."

Contract Administrator: "ID, money, jacket, rain gear, and cellular phone."

Retired Auto Worker: "The least absolutely necessary for the trip."

Pastor: "When I was a biker, I was known to carry cash, beer or wine, and a pistol."

HD Salesman: "As little as possible."

Teacher: "As much as I can fit into my garbage wagon."

Teacher: "Whatever I'll need for the ride; as it depends on the destination and purpose. But I always carry money, basic tools, leathers, and a knife."

Funeral Director: "I leave the guns at home so I don't shoot the MFers in 4-wheelers who cut me off!"

Motorcycle Safety Foundation Rider Coach: "Maps, sunglasses, rain gear, warmer clothes, registration and insurance cards, cellular, water, camera, First Aid Kit, emergency tools, flashlight, and sidestand puck. More stuff than I thought!"

Motorcycle Safety Foundation Rider Coach: "I carry lots of stuff that most bikers carry; so I'll just add one that most wish they had: GPS!"

Retired Non-Biker: "Helmet! Helmet! Helmet!"

Administrative Assistant: "I think of some things that others seem to forget like a tire gauge, zip lock waterproof bags, spare bulbs, fuses, air pump, and little shit that become major deals if you're caught without them."

While I think the best lists of the basics to carry for the ride are in Jay Barbieri's *Biker's Handbook* and the Motorcycle Safety Foundation's *Basic Rider Course Rider Handbook* (2009), you learn as you go. It's like the exchange between the older biker and the younger one in Pirsig's bestseller:

> *"How did you know how to do that?" he asks.*
>
> *"You just have to figure it out."*
>
> *It's a transferable metaphor: Not everyone understands what a completely rational process this is, this maintenance of a motorcycle. They think it's some kind of a "knack" or some kind of "affinity for machines" in operation... A motorcycle functions entirely in accordance with the laws of reason, and a study of the art of motorcycle maintenance is really a miniature study of the art of rationality itself.*

The basic of all basics, of course, for a biker is the bike itself.

Stock (fresh from the manufacturer and off the shelf) or chopped (stripped down – *chopped* - to its barest essentials), the bike, Garripoli notes, "becomes a mirror that reflects the whole of my life."

Thompson got it right: "...their bikes as personal monuments, created in their own image, however abstract, and they develop an affection for them that is hard for outsiders to understand."

God knows it borders on *and sometimes crosses over into* idolatry; distracting the affections and allegiance due God alone. It's akin to saying, "I just worship *her, him,* or *whomever/whatever.*"

Indeed, I've seen some bikers who fondle their bikes a lot more than their mates; but, of course, some will retort that their bikes are a lot more responsive than their mates.

There's also a lot of arrogance in the biker world about *makes.*

While I prefer HDs over all other makes for patriotic as well as performance reasons – I refuse to feed the coffers of countries who dump their products into our market while employing unfair trade and labor practices and I just like the way my HD sounds, looks, feels, and rides! – I will wave to the metrics and even the crotch rocketeers who seem more into show and speed than the aesthetics and metaphysics of riding.

God knows the pathetic parallel in the church; as one franchise/denomination feels so much superior to another and churchgoers talk more about being Baptist, Lutheran, Methodist, Presbyterian, or Roman Catholic that being *Christian.*

Just as being a Christian has a lot more to do with the behavior of the believer than institutional affiliation and just as being a biker has a lot more to do with the biker's ride than the bike's make, the metaphor is transferable because *who you are* matters so much more than *what you have.*

Who you are more than anything else determines the authenticity of *who you claim to be.*

An authentic Christian loves Jesus by loving like Jesus; proclaiming and practicing the Psalmist's profession, "Your word is a lamp for my feet and a light on my path."

An authentic biker doesn't think about another biker's bike's *make* nearly as much as the shared experience of the ride.

Only inauthentics care about the small stuff.

While authentics may have personal preferences, those preferences don't become prejudices to segregate and separate from other riders.

Again, it's *who you are* more than *what you have* that exposes authenticity or inauthenticity.

I'll never forget going on one of my favorite rides from Wilkes-Barre, Pennsylvania to Bar Harbor, Maine back in the early 70s.

I broke down on Route 81 just north of Scranton; which means things had started poorly. I thought things were going from poorly to catastrophically when a pack of Pagans stopped; because back in those days, they rode HDs mostly and Triumphs if necessary. There I was on the side of the road with my little shiny red Honda 350 Four and just about pooping my pants as their bikes thundered to a halt as one especially burly mountain of a man with more hair than I've ever had on almost every part of his mostly exposed body demanded, "What's wrong with your pony, boy?"

Before I could explain that I had no idea what was wrong other than I was broken down on the side of the road with a bunch of the most notorious outlaw 1%ers gathered for anything but prayer, a couple of 'em jumped off their bikes, tore into mine, got it running, and then rode off with the trailer scolding, "I'd get rid of that piece of Jap shit and get a real mule if you're goin' anywhere other than round the block near mama's house!"

I don't think I've experienced many better incarnations of the parable of the good Samaritan.

Certainly, there are so many reasons why people ride.

Getting back to the survey:

Pastor: "It clears my head of clutter and all of the crap that I deal with daily in my congregation."

Teacher: "It makes me feel so alive."

Policeman: "I like the camaraderie with other bikers; even the ones I arrest when in uniform."

CEO: "It's my escape from all of my worries."

Pastor: "It's easy to get around town, easy parking, and I save a lot of money on gas."

Homemaker: "Cheaper than a psychiatrist."

Retired Steel Worker: "I escape high gas prices, congested roads, noxious fumes, and most traffic jams. I ride the back roads so I don't have to deal with as many folks who spoil the ride because there in such a hurry to get somewhere."

Pastor: “I never ride when I’m in a hurry. I ride to stop hurrying. I like to ride slow. I like to savor the sights and smells. It’s my therapy. I tell people that it’s dangerous to ride if you’re in a hurry. I guess you could say that for everything else too.”

Lawyer: “I connect with my surroundings.”

My son Matthew: “It’s such a thrill. Awesome!”

Veno says it for me:

... the motorcycle has attracted those who love the freedom of the open road... an adrenaline rush that cannot be fathomed by car drivers. The concentration required to operate a motorcycle blocks all bullshit from your mind, focusing attention on the near-addictive high of riding. If motorcycles influence your life, then you are part of the motorcycling community.

I’m with Jay Leno:

The first bike I ever got was a Honda 350 back in 1971... You didn’t have to have a license in those days... I remember getting on the freeway, not knowing what I was doing... But I still remember thinking, “This is fun!”

It’s so basic.

Fun.

Again, it's a transferable metaphor.

Jesus came to fill us with joy: "I have come so that my joy may be in you!"

Jesus never came to lead a funeral procession.

He came, as He said, that we might have life *and have it abundantly!*

A lot of churchgoers seem to miss that.

A lot of churchgoers look like they're stuck in the mud of monotonous low-life existence.

They look bored.

I've never seen a biker looking bored while riding; and I've never seen an authentic Jesus-lover looking bored because riding with Jesus is overcoming *death* and everything/everyone else that tries to kill the life in us.

A homemaker responded to the survey, "Bikers are big time party*ers*!"

Well, I've got news for you!

Jesus was a big time party*er*!

They ran out of wine at that first wedding and Jesus made more; and His was better than their best!

When He showed up at the birth of the church as the Holy Spirit, nobody twiddled their thumbs!

They jumped up and down and danced and sang and had so much fun!

There's an old story about the pastor who slipped in prayer, "And, O Lord, if the fires of faith are stoked this morning and flames of passion dart in every direction, water those sparks!"

So many churchgoers remind me of little Dougie Watson standing next to his mom at the end of worship in the sanctuary of Clark, New Jersey's Osceola Presbyterian Church over 30 years ago. I announced the closing hymn, he turned the page, and lamented, "Just my luck! Six verses!"

I'll never forget meeting my mother-in-law for the first time at Pittsburgh International Airport. I love her a lot; because she convinced me to marry Leslie when she said, "All Leslie wants to do is have fun."

I said, "Excellent!"

It's so basic.

We ride for the fun of it!

FTW.

Robert R. Kopp

Clubs

Most churches suffer fools gladly.

Their membership standards for admittance and discipline of continuing members are so weak that mobocracy reigns regardless of polity; allowing anybody's word to be as good as everybody else's word on anything without respect to education, expertise, or experience.

A very old pastor in a nursing home, a predecessor in my first church, explained it this way: "Just one flea can make a big dog itch." Or as my friend Jan likes to say, "Some people are like farts in the elevator. It takes just one. Everyone suffers. Nobody escapes."

I've seen so many opportunities flow in, through, and out of churches because one or two *players* pitch a fit about it; longing for the way things never were or maybe were but are no more which doesn't really matter anyway because *they're* against it if they haven't thought of it first.

Or something like that.

Harry and Vic come to mind.

I met Harry in my first church as an ordained pastor (viz., First Presbyterian Church, Parkesburg, Pennsylvania).

Incidentally/parenthetically/providentially, a lot of Pagans liked to hang out in Parkesburg.

Though it was a long time ago when I was so much more *Like a Rock,* I often return to my confrontation with Harry, fears about it, and how the outcome has proven to be a tonic over the years as I recall it for pastors in distress or even me when I'm, uh, distressed.

Be that as it is because of how it was and will usually be, Harry was the biggest giver in the church and made sure we knew it, president of the trustees who thought they/*Harry* were/was in control, and had a spiritually nauseating way of reminding everyone of how important he was to the survival of the church and how we could never get along without him which he threatened so regularly whenever anyone questioned him or dared propose something that he hadn't thought of first.

So people yielded to every one of Harry's self-ordained prerogatives and walked on eggshells around him for fear of saying or doing anything that would provoke his ire or exit.

Whenever I think of Harry and people like him, I recall Martin Luther King, Jr.'s sermon on *The Drum Major Instinct* (2/4/68, Ebenezer Baptist Church, Atlanta, Georgia):

> *There is, deep down within all of us, an instinct. It's a kind of drum major instinct – a desire to be out front, a desire to lead the parade, a desire to be first... And you know, we begin early to ask life to put us first. Our first cry as a baby was a bid for attention... Children ask life to grant them first place. They are a little bundle of ego... Now in adult life, we still have it... We like to be praised for it.*

It's like a friend relayed to me in quoting a mentor, "You can't always count on God's children to act Godly; but you can always count on them to act like children."

*Be **that** as it is,* the session of my first church, elected elders or leaders who really run the church as the highest ruling body in my particular ecclesiastical franchise no matter what anybody else presumes, voted to restore the sidewalk on the east side of the sanctuary with cement not long after I arrived.

The vote was unanimous.

But not long after that, a city work crew showed up and started blacktopping the sidewalk.

I rushed out: “What are you doing?”

Answer: “Well, Harry told us to blacktop your sidewalks because we’ve got some leftovers from patching the streets.”

Moi: “You can’t do that because session voted to use cement.”

Answer: “Listen, boy, when Harry tells us to do something, we do it. That’s the way it is around here.”

King:

> *Nobody is unhappy when they are praised, even if they know they don’t deserve it, and even if they don’t believe it. The only unhappy people about praise is when that praise is going too much toward somebody else... If this instinct is not harnessed, it becomes very dangerous, pernicious... really... [becoming]... sickening because they just sit up all the time talking about themselves. And they just boast, and boast, and... it causes one to engage ultimately in activities that are merely used to get attention... leads to snobbish exclusivism... I’ve known churches get in that bind sometimes...*

I went back into the church and called my executive presbyter (akin to a bishop as counselor to pastors in her/his jurisdiction and enforcer of the franchise’s rules) who said after I dumped the dirty details, “You go back out there right now and tell them that session not Harry makes decisions in your church.”

I asked timidly, “Can you repeat that?”

He did; then I did.

They stopped.

Harry came storming into the church in less than ten minutes, pointed his finger in my face, and screamed, "I don't care what you or that session or your book of rules says. We're blacktopping the sidewalk."

"Harry," I said while trying not to appear as afraid as I was, "I don't run this church and you don't run this church. Session makes decisions and I make sure they're followed. If you tell them to blacktop the sidewalk, I will have to call the police."

Not long after that, Harry left the church.

King:

> *Oh, I see you want to be first... You want to be significant. Well, you ought to be. If you're going to be... [His]... my disciple, you must be... Yes, don't give up this instinct. It's a good instinct if you use it right. It's a good instinct if you don't distort it and pervert it. Don't give it up. Keep feeling the need for being important. Keep feeling the need for being first... But I want you to be first in love. I want you to be first in moral excellence. I want you to be first in generosity...*

Harry's two sons who were on the session at the time called for a special meeting.

I started updating my dossier.

I was so afraid.

I opened the meeting with an incoherent prayer; and the oldest of the two sons said, "Thank you, pastor, for reminding our father that the church was here before he came and will be here after he leaves. Thank you for reminding us that the church is about a people working together for the Lord and not about persons getting their own way. I wasn't sure you were the right pastor for us until now."

I could hear the apostle in the distance: "We each have different work to do. We belong to each other. Each needs all of the others... for the common good."

I heard Harry's boys picked him up during a Christmas Day family meal, carried him outside, and threw him into a pile of snow.

I thought that was funny, then sad, then funny, and then sad.

As for the church, it grew and grew and grew; and we never had money problems again.

Gardeners refer to it as pruning – painful but necessary for growth.

Vic was a lot more sophisticated than Harry.

I met him at the height of my fame as an ecclesiastical boy wonder when he was approaching the height of his fame as the most prolific car dealer in the Triad of North Carolina.

While he was too rich to tithe, he was exceptionally generous to the church and community; and he would always say within moments of getting together with me, "Now if there's anything you need..."

About a year into my ministry at that church, he came in and said, "I'm very distressed because my good friend Phoebe is leaving the church because she just doesn't like you. I'd like you to meet with her and see if you can work things out."

I met with her.

She was a distinguished Southern belle; and there wasn't any room in her world for a Yankee like me; and it didn't help when I repeated a favorite line whenever somebody in that church tried to control me: "Hey, I know you're used to ownin' people down here *but...*"

Yankees!

So I called Vic with my report; and after saying she was gonna leave because she kinda loathed me *in a Christian kinda way,* I noted, "It's just like your business, Vic. You sell more cars than anybody else in the Triad; but, still, some folks prefer to shop elsewhere. We've got a flood of new people coming into the church; but, just like your business, there's a trickle out who don't like our products."

Then Vic said something that has stayed with me ever since as the sobering reality of ecclesiastical *clubbiness* that often counters the Founder's inclusive intention for the church along with His expectation that people who love Him will love like Him and not let incidental idiosyncrasies inhibit unity through and for Him amid the divinely ordered diversity of His people, "I really don't care about them. All I care about is my friend is leaving the church because of you."

Vic wasn't really thinking about the lost coin, sheep, or son; but rather his one friend whose departure was more important to him than the throng who were entering.

Both Harry and Vic meant well; but both failed to see the whole is bigger than any of its parts.

Though he meant well, Harry wanted to control everybody because he really believed he knew "better" than anybody else about everything.

But that's not how God planned it.

He planned interdependence (read Romans 12 and 1 Corinthians 12).

Harry had to go because he was a singular barrier to the blessings of God flowing through others to enrich the church.

Pruning.

Though he meant well, Vic didn't care about the many who were coming in because of the one who was leaving.

But that's not how God planned it.

As the apostle Paul enlightened his student Timothy, "God wants everybody to be saved."

In other words, if the church doesn't make room for everybody, there's no longer enough room for those who want to restrict expansion.

Phoebe had to go because her prejudices precluded the notorious inclusion for which the Founder was famous (read John 3:16).

Harry and Vic provided pret' near perfect examples of two paradoxes in the church.

God wants everybody to have a say in His club/church *except for those who don't want anybody else to have a say.*

God wants everybody in His club/church *except for those who don't want everybody in His club/church.*

Bikers seem to understand that a lot more than churchgoers.

While no one is immune to the herd mentality with its mobocratic behaviors, farmers are right: "Always drink upstream from the herd."

Unlike too many of today's churches in which anybody's word is as good as everybody else's word on anything without respect to education, expertise, or experience *because* of weak membership standards for admittance and weak discipline of continuing members, biker clubs, for the most part, have very strict membership standards and exercise very strict discipline of continuing members to maintain those membership standards.

While *authentic* churches will require its members to believe in Jesus as Lord and Savior and behave like they believe He is Lord and Savior, *inauthentic* versions allow admittance and continuing membership with standards best described as *laissez-faire*.

Most biker clubs have very strict standards for admittance; requiring a certain kind of bike, mandatory attendance as designated *with no exceptions,* mandatory dues *with no exceptions,* and a loyalty to each other individually as part of the corporate pledge *with no exceptions*.

Most biker clubs are puzzled to scorn by churches that keep "inactive" membership rolls for those who are undecided about their roles in particular churches; asserting you're either "for us" or "against us" which sounds very close to something that the Founder of the Church required for membership.

Biker clubs demand a loyalty from its members that causes envy in churches; or as 81er Mike North, who lives in the shadow of the church that I serve now, reported, "People I thought were my friends and brothers weren't... People in Hells Angels, whether they like me or not, will back me up if something happens to me..."

John Hall's commendation of the loyalty among Pagans is reflected in most biker clubs: "The Pagans learned... that one righteous brother willing to go down for the club was worth 10 hangers-on who were only looking for cheap thrills and loose women."

Again, that sounds like what Jesus expected from people who gather in churches who claim Him as the Leader of their pack: "People who say they love Me must deny themselves, take up their cross, and follow Me... There is no greater love than to die for your friends..."

Dave Nichols captures the devotional attitude of authentics to their clubs: "He is the kid who pushes back – he might not win every fight but he won't put up with any crap. The rebel... has a very low tolerance for bullshit of any kind" (*One Percenter,* 2007.)

Simply, biker clubs, unlike too many churches, don't suffer fools gladly; or as a schoolteacher added at the bottom of her survey, "I like bikers. They are loyal to each other and kind to most people... yet capable of kickin' ass."

1%ers come to mind.

While there are some who claim to be authentic 1%ers but are really just criminals who ride bikes, just like there are people on the dark side who are messing up things in so many churches, 1%ers represent that small percentage of authenticity that are part of biking and even Christianity at His best.

I've been spending a lot of time with an authentic 1%er who has been burned by so many inauthentic Christians in the past that he still loves Jesus while having little time or patience for many churches. He explained:

> *I am a 1%er... We are not only a societal sub-culture, but a sub-culture within the biker community. We are often shunned or avoided...*
>
> *Contrary to reputation... we are not a bunch of criminals, drug abusers, hell-raisers... We have families that we love and care for... We go to work every day. We obey the laws that are fair and just. Granted, every "outlaw" club has a few bad elements and we do not condone their behavior... [He has chronicled several instances for me of members who were kicked out of the club for violating club rules; which is so unlike so many churches that won't even kick out members who don't acknowledge Jesus as Lord and Savior!]...*

What causes us to be painted with the same brush as the bad elements is due to the fact that we love our brothers dearly and are there for them even when they screw up... and believe me, we let them know when they are wrong. We can be very firm with those we love. We want them to be well... and as long as they want to be well, they're in the club...

We are a complex group with a lot of nuances. It's interesting to us that the "weekend warriors" are parrots of each other trying to imitate what they think we are about. They do this with their attire, attitude, speech, and actions; often to a degree that is very funny to us... [Of course, we have joked of the parallel in so many churches!]...

The individuals in our clubs are just that – individuals. This is very important to us... Weekend warriors have their role. They have become so prolific in number that they deflect attention away from us; which is good. They have made it very hard for society and authorities to differentiate them from us...

Perhaps "Christians" are a lot like this.

I've always contended that anyone can be a Christian for two hours a week, walk out the church door after worship and go back to habits which are not Christlike. I have some

Christian friends who truly live like Scriptural Christians. These people have my undying respect.

From time to time, I've been asked by the weekend guys why someone would want to be in a club like mine. Usually, I'll size up the person asking and most times walk away. When I do realize that the person asking is sincere and non-judgmental, I will try to explain the brotherhood, commitment, love, and respect we have for each other...

Churches seem to accept just about anyone as members today.

1%ers are not like that. We have higher standards. It's a long process before one patches out or becomes a full patch member...

1%ers work harder. We are always conscious of the example we are setting for new or younger members, the work it takes sometimes to love and support a brother who has screwed up, to take every penny you have to help a club brother who has fallen on hard times, and to conduct yourself in a manner that will not bring any disrespect to the patch or the club...

That's why I refer to authentic 1%ers as 100%ers – totally committed to being the best of who they claim to be. Yeah, they may be only 1% of the biker/Christian population; but they're 100% committed to it/Him: "You gotta be 100% committed to being known as the outlaw 1% who won't follow or conform to mainstream society" (81er).

Veno explained the passionate commitment of membership to a biker club that is rarely seen in churches: "Most clubs have a long, arduous process of admission and members must adhere to strict rules to maintain their membership... The person must... develop into what... bikers call a 'righteous biker' – committed to the biker lifestyle."

Randy Stonehill sings about the difference between authentics and inauthentics in both cultures:

Keep me runnin' from the shadow of my lies
Like a gypsy who is never satisfied
Once you compromise your soul
You spend a lifetime dodging the devil's toll

While convinced biker clubs do a better job than most churches in inviting, welcoming, including, and loving people regardless of class, color, or culture, some biker clubs, as already acknowledged, are false witnesses to the highest values of the biker culture.

Some bikers are as bigoted about women and race as some ultra-right wing nutballs masquerading as followers of Jesus; but, for the most part, John Hall is right: bikers are "more concerned with *who you are* than *what you are."*

Authentics are patriotic.

When I went to buy a helmet at a big HD sale for those forays into the danger zones of travel, I found one that was reduced from $140 to $40. It was a premium helmet; and as I've said before, HD may mean *high dollar* yet you can always count on the unsurpassed quality of HD products. My only hesitancy was that it was covered with eagles and flames and I thought it looked a little cheesy.

When I mentioned that to the saleswoman, she said, "Take a look! Bikers are into America! They're the real freedom fighters of today! They cherish freedom and that's what America is supposed to be all about. So you'll see more eagles and flags and patriotic patches on bikers than just about anybody else!"

It's true.

And it's true that authentic Christians are into everything that points to Jesus by symbol and utterance.

My favorite devotional writer, Ella Jane Coley of Passageway Ministries in Bixby, Oklahoma, wrote about this authenticity among His people:

> *There are wars going on in the churches! Where peace, unity, and love once flowed, the atmosphere is now charged with strife, confusion, and division. We can barely get along with members of our own congregations, much less Christians of different congregations... Beloved, we are called to peace and love, joy and gladness, and to be each other's burden-bearers!... When saints begin to fight for each other and not against one another, even hell trembles... It's time we fight for one another!*

That means being 100% committed even if you're only 1% of the population.

My friend with the "I Am My Brother's Keeper!" patch under his back collar comes to mind again.

Authentic bikers stand up, speak up, and act up for each other.

Authentic churchgoers look up to Jesus, stand up for Jesus, speak up for Jesus, and act up for Jesus; and when they're doing that, it blesses others because blessing others is the same as blessing Him:

"Love each other *just as much as* I have loved you!... When you love each other, people will know you love Me!"

Another Randy Stonehill song comes to mind:

I've got news for you.
This is not a game!

Everybody's going to the movies.
Everybody's leaving for the show.
Seems as if we've lost the nerve for feeling.
And no one's in the mood to want to know.

I've got news for you.
This is not a game!

I've got news for you.
Are you listening?

I've got news for you.
We're all the same!

I've got news for you.
We're all to blame!

When that is understood,
We can start to live again!

I agree with Pirsig: "I think that if we are going to reform the world, and make it a better place to live in... The place to improve the world is first in one's own heart and head and hands, and then work outward from there."

Getting back to patches, there are two that are righteous *if you know what they really mean* but vulgar *if you're ignorant and inauthentic.*

FTW ("Fuck the world!") means I'm not going to let anyone or anything distract me from being authentic!

DILLIGAF ("Do I Look Like I Give a Fuck?") means I don't really care what inauthentics think because I'm trying to be authentic!

That's how authentic biker clubs feel and act.

That's authentic churches feel and act.

They just wanna ride.

FTW.

Robert R. Kopp

Weather

Ed meant well.

Whenever I say something like that, I think of my dad who always likes to say, "The road to hell is paved with good intentions."

Be that as it may be, Ed meant well.

I met him about 30 years ago in New Jersey when I was pastor of Clark's Osceola Presbyterian Church.

Ed was one of those annoying kinda guys who always shadowed me in an idolatrous kinda way. Though it's kinda nice to have someone slobbering over you when you know there are others conspiring around corners for an ambush, it wears out after a while because idolatry is always wrong and all idols fall and fail sooner or later. That's why I tell people with Chuck Colson, "Don't follow me! Follow Jesus!" I know I just can't rise to every occasion like He did/can/will. I'm not into posing; and I'm still into Edie's song.

Speaking of slobbering, Ed was a real scumbag. I'm not being critical. That's just a fact. He always had something drooling out of the corners of his mouth and always had something hanging from his nose and he was always picking at his teeth or nose or ears or eyes or crotch and his hair was always greasy and he always had dandruff flakes all over his shirt that were bigger than antependia for Easter Day and he always brought *Animal House*'s Babs to mind – "That boy is a P-I-G pig!" – at church potlucks.

Then he died suddenly.

His wife Dotty was a nurse. She was everything that Ed was not: cultured, clean, and performing as well as meaning well.

When we met to plan Ed's funeral, I was kinda struck by the bright colors that she was wearing and a giddiness that didn't seem especially in keeping with the occasion; but despite still being green behind the ears and only a few years out of seminary, I already knew people grieved in different ways.

But when she burst out in laughter as I prayed for Jesus to comfort and console her in such a great loss, I had to ask, "Dotty, I know people grieve in different ways; but I've never seen someone so seemingly happy at such a time as this."

Smiling, she said, "Oh, Bob, I feel so free and relieved. He was so disgusting. We've been married *forever;* and it was so awful. Let me tell you how awful it was. Whenever I would give in to him and have sex with him just so I could get away from him when it was over, I would run into the bathroom after it was all over, vomit, and then scrub myself clean in the shower."

I've presided at hundreds of memorial services since then; but not even the widows with someone in the wings smiled as broadly while singing those dirges.

"Into every life," we often hear, "a little rain must fall."

No one is immune; for as Jesus said, "The rain falls on everybody."

Sometimes it feels like a downpour.

A friend, who is an elder in the church where I'm currently pastor, and I know what that's all about.

In early spring 2009 just after Easter Day, we traveled from Belvidere, Illinois through Milwaukee, Wisconsin to just south of Green Bay to visit another elder who had a stroke and was confined to a nursing home. It took three hours to get there in clear and seasonably warm weather. It took seven hours to get back as the weather patterns shifted and we were hit with rain, sleet, hale, and unseasonably cold weather that confirmed our suspicions about Al Gore's pontifications on global warming.

Our bikes were up to it – HDs! – but we were totally unprepared for it; bringing a biker adage to mind: "The only good view of a thunderstorm is in your rear view mirror."

Neither of us packed rain gear for the trip or extra *anything*.

We learned a powerful lesson that we should have picked up from Boy Scouts: "Be prepared!"

A wife and her husband asleep in bed ring a bell.

Awakened by the telephone, the husband answers, "Hello? How do I know? Do you think I'm a weatherman?"

And he slammed down the phone.

"What was that?" his wife asked.

He answered, "I don't have a clue. It was somebody wanting to know if the coast was clear."

Bad weather is a biker's next to worst nightmare.

But with the reality of weather reports being as reliable as a Democrats' commitment to capitalism, it's best to prepare for the worst.

Surely, the best advice comes from the farm: "Life is simpler when you plow around the stump."

If the weather is gonna be awful, keep the mule in the barn!

But knowing you're gonna get caught sooner or later and more often than not, having a bike in good repair, carrying clothing for changing conditions, and adapting plans as appropriate is how to *weather* it all.

On the other hand, sometimes the rain that falls has nothing to do with the climate; and turning to Walt Disney's *Bambi* (1942), we discover the greatest threat to a biker's safety. Bambi asked his mother, "What happened mother? Why did we all run?" She answered, "Man was in the forest."

The biggest threat to bikers is not the thunderstorm in the rear view mirror. It's who/what requires more than what can be stored in saddlebags; or as one company has printed on their mirror heads: "ASSHOLES IN MIRROR ARE BIGGER THAN THEY APPEAR."

There are a lot of scumbags out there who bring storms into your life.

Craig Bourne wrote (*Philosophical Ridings: Motorcycles and the Meaning of Life,* 2007): "Even if riders are fully confident of their own abilities and that of their motorcycles, it's not possible to guarantee that the rest of the world won't stuff things up."

Then he gets specific: "Everyone needs to be protected from thoughtless idiots who race around the streets endangering others."

Admittedly, I'm thinking mostly of cages with four or more wheels; but even bikers know other bikers who give a bad name to them.

More than less, however, bikers – crotch rocketers being the exception – are not the primary culprits or predators to their safety. Mike Myers, President of the Kishwaukee Valley A.B.A.T.E. (A Brotherhood Aimed Toward Education) in Illinois, roared: "It seems... the media and... Illinois are hell bent to give ALL bikers a hard time. All we want to do is to be left alone and enjoy our rides" (*Kickstart,* July 2009).

He asked, "Why is it whenever there is a motorcycle accident they want to make sure that everyone knows that they were not wearing a helmet?... What message do you think most non-riders think?"

Sarcastically, he answered his own questions: "If you wear a helmet you are invincible and can ride as stupid as you wish and you will never be hurt or die... No other vehicle will pull out in front of you... No other vehicle will try to share your lane and run you off of the road... No other vehicle will run you over while doing their nails, reading the paper or text-messaging."

Responses in the survey to the related question – "What is the biggest threat to a biker's safety?" – were surprisingly consistent among bikers and non-bikers. Though all agreed there are bikers who are dangerous, irresponsible, and the like, most cite other vehicular drivers as the biggest threats to bikers' safety; though a response from a UAW mechanical engineer was the most creative: "Republicans are the biggest threat whether in their steel cages or as the driving force behind legislation against bikers!"

Experienced bikers can handle most weather conditions; and if necessary, they just stop and wait for things to clear up.

Experienced bikers can handle the human elements as well; and if necessary, they just stop and let 'em pass.

All bikers know most accidents occur when *caution* yields to *hurry*.

But, again, the greatest defense against all opponents – storms or scumbags – is building a solid foundation of preparation; for the bad weather will come and no one is immune to it.

Jesus put it best: "The wise man builds his house on a solid rock foundation; so he survives the winds and rain and bad weather of life."

Ron Hutchcraft wrote about overcoming bad weather in a devotional on November 26, 2008:

> *Some of us have had some very strange winters with wild temperature swings between unseasonably warm, and then sudden drops to very cold and back again... Out of those rapid changes come some less than fun driving conditions like black ice... There's a snowstorm or ice storm one day, and then it's warm enough the next day to*

start melting much or most of that frozen stuff. Then it gets cold again at night, and what thawed during the day freezes at night, sometimes into this dark invisible ice patch on the street –that's black ice.

He continued,

Now, a lot of good people have ended up sliding into a spiritual accident the same way... You're speeding along, carelessly assuming that you won't crash and that's where Satan lays down a patch of his black ice – a carefully crafted opportunity to sin that totally blindsides you and suddenly, you have slidden into damage you could have never imagined.

His conclusion is about the preparations for our biggest threat to safety:

That's why our word for today from the Word of God needs to be reinforced regularly in our minds... "Be self-controlled and alert"... Make sure you're letting Jesus drive you on that hazardous road ahead and don't take back the wheel when it looks like the road is totally safe. Your enemy always has places for you to slip, and Jesus will make sure you swerve to miss the black ice of sin's surprises.

Again, no one avoid the storms, scumbags, and Satanic strategies of life; but we can overcome them by preparing for them.

Practically, we do everything in our power to increase the odds of a safe ride.

Spiritually, we rely on His power to guarantee a safe ride.

It's like one of my preaching professors used to counsel, "Trust Jesus; and, in everything else, hang loose!"

The only way to beat the weather with all of its storms and scumbags and Satanic strategies is to do our best and trust God for the differences.

I like those odds a lot more than riding on my own.

Robert R. Kopp

Curses

A pastor who always wanted a convertible and finally saved up enough money to buy one was confronted by an officer of his church: "Your predecessor had one. We got rid of him. We think a convertible presents a bad image for our pastor. So you can't buy one."

While confessing to my peer that I'm probably not the best guy to address vehicular images, I counseled, "I can think of four reasons why you should buy one: (1) You want one and have enough money to buy one; (2) You're almost as old as I am which means you could keel over at any moment which means it's now or maybe never; (3) Once you allow people to control any part of your life, they'll feel entitled to control all of your life; and (4) People, especially in the church these days, are always looking for something to bitch and moan about when it comes to their pastors; so I think you should buy one and give them something to talk about before they make up or come up something else to bitch and moan about it."

While the Bible says we have been created in "the image of God" which means we have been predestined to the apex of His created order with an allowance for holy communion with Him and gifted with thoughts, time, talents, and treasures to honor Him, there are more than enough people who want to make up our minds for us about just about everything; or as I've relayed to more than a few folks who've tried it with me over the years, "I won't judge myself because there are so many who like to do that for me."

Too many people have this dark assumption about having some kinda divine right to tell us who we are and how we feel and what we should and should not be doing.

In short, people have this inclination to *should* on each other.

I'm reminded of a conversation between Freud and Jung. Jung said, "You've said cigars are phallic symbols." As he inhaled deeply from his stogie, Freud replied, "You're right; but they're also cigars."

Bikers understand their "image" problems; and whether it's an unjustified connection with criminals (God knows there are more criminals who drive Chevys than motorcycles!) or accusation that they're riding around on their manhood (God knows the same could be said about guns, knives, fishing rods, personalized bowling balls, the latest oversized drivers from Callaway, big screens, crackberries, and all of the rest!) or something else as equally inane, bikers seem to evoke more pejorative passions from non-bikers than just about any other group in our culture.

Bikers are "cursed" by images imposed upon them.

Though comparing the sacrifice of Jesus and the martyrs is a stretch, there is one important parallel. *Everyone who did/does not fit into the prevailing cultural images of their times were/are targets for those who assumed/assume – That word again! – they were/are the arbiters of all true faith and morality.* Hence, Jesus predicted for anyone who steps outside of cultural images, "You will have suffering in this world."

While I've had as much psychotherapeutic education and experience as many shrinks who get megabucks for what I do as a part of my service to the church, I don't pretend to know *for certain* why bikers have an especially elevated status in the disdain of our purveyors of political correctness. I have two guesses: (1) the insatiable lust to control and compel others to conform to their way of life; and (2) jealousy.

Getting back to *Easy Rider,* the campfire scene illustrates the profound bipolarity of our culture when it comes to individual freedom juxtaposed to cultural control needs:

George: "You know, this used to be a helluva good country. I can't understand what's gone wrong with it."

Billy: "Huh. Man, everybody got chicken. That's what happened, man. Hey, we can't even get into like, a, second-rate hotel. I mean, a second-rate motel. You dig? They think we're gonna cut their throat or something, man. They're scared, man."

George: "Oh, they're not scared of you. They're scared of what you represent to 'em."

Billy: "Hey, man. All we represent to them, man, is somebody who needs a haircut."

George: "Oh, no. What you represent to them is freedom."

Billy: "What the hell's wrong with freedom, man? That's what it's all about."

George: "Oh, yeah, that's right. That's what it's all about, all right. But talkin' about it and bein' it... that's two different things. I mean, it's real hard to be free when you are bought and sold in the marketplace. 'Course, don't ever tell anybody that they're not free 'cause then they're gonna get real busy killin' and maimin' to prove to you that they are. Oh, yeah, they're gonna talk to you, and talk to you, and talk to you about individual freedom, but they see a free individual, it's gonna scare 'em."

Billy: "Hmm. Well, that don't make 'em runnin' scared."

George: "No, it makes 'em dangerous."

I can't resist telling you about the nervous bride who said to her pastor during the wedding rehearsal, "I just don't know what I'm supposed to do and when I'm supposed to do it." The pastor said, "It's simple: just walk down the aisle to the altar and we'll sing a hymn."

She said, "O.K., I think I've got it: aisle... altar... hymn."

If it were that superficial and silly, folks like Wyatt, Billy, George, and countless others wouldn't have been blown away from the culture by the makers, guardians, and accommodators of the *machine*.

Unfortunately, Dave Nichols is right on: "Today we live in a restrictive Big Brother society in which the nanny state rules over our every move. We cannot drive a car without wearing a seatbelt; we cannot ride a motorcycle without wearing a helmet; we cannot cross the street anywhere except in areas clearly marked for crossing."

Mark R. Levin refers to them as "Statists" (*aka* socialists) in *Liberty and Tyranny* (2009), "...the Statist is building a culture of conformity and dependency, where the ideal citizen takes on dronelike qualities in service to the state, the individual must be drained of uniqueness and self-worth, and deterred from independent thought or behavior."

Begging your indulgence for my vocational ghetto's experience, which has parallels in too many others, a friend in Oklahoma wrote, "A local pastor's wife passed away after a long illness. He decided to get a chrome pony; and it actually split the church. It seems the congregation just couldn't handle their pastor enjoying something that wasn't dignified according to their standards."

A good friend and my predecessor in Belvidere explained the justification/rationalization used by controlling *interests:* "Sometimes even people who love Jesus cannot distinguish between His words and theirs. They begin to think what they say is what He would say. They become messianic."

It's the bastardization of the Biblical understanding of being created *in the image of God:* "So man created God! In the image of man, man created God!"

People look into the mirror and see Jesus; or, at least, they act that way.

That's what gives them the "right" to control others.

It sounds crazy.

It is.

But I think it's why some people think they're entitled to control other people according to their *images*.

I'm reminded of my first year in seminary. I told the registrar that I'd probably be a more effective pastor if I took Spanish instead of Hebrew or Greek. He said, "You can take Spanish *in addition to Hebrew and Greek.*" When I asked why, he said, "Because I had to..."

Jealousy also seems to provide the energy behind non-bikers' antagonism.

I cannot tell you how often I've watched from the window of a coffee shop or fast food joint as someone a little younger, my age, or a little older looked so longingly at my parked pony with the clear betrayal, "Geez! I wish I had the guts *and freedom* to ride one of these!"

Somebody sent these lines from J.R. Rooney and L.J. James to me that appeared in an unknown source:

> *Whenever a person or group of people try to live their lives free, those who are stuck in unhappy lives will be jealous...*
>
> *There is something about riding a bike that inspires a sense of freedom in me. The open road, wind in my face, the smells, getting back to nature, the power of the bike. It's all these things and more that make me feel free. It's unfortunate that there are some people who... can't find something or someway to let go and experience the sense of freedom that we do. These people... are the ones who point to us and call us rogues or rebels...*
>
> *Don't hate these envious people, pity them for they will never know the sense of freedom and brotherhood we get from riding... They'll never know the wind in their face, the feeling of peace and oneness with nature we feel... They'll never know the clarity of mind that comes from a long ride... Just thank your higher power that you've found a way to escape, a way to be free...*

I feel sorry for those jealously controlling people almost as much as I feel sorry for people who reject the existential and eternal securities of Jesus.

Sadly, a black judge and black Pepsi distributor in Toledo, Ohio helped me to understand the roots of that jealousy and lust for control. While playing golf with them, I complained about a black woman in the church hating me *just because* I'm white. Simultaneously, they blurted out the truth: "She's just ignorant!"

Of course, that doesn't help when some moron in a four-or-more-wheeled machine cuts you off or drives you off the road; and when you catch a glimpse of 'em, you see menacing demons racing all over their faces.

Knowing why they're so inconsiderate of your safety – *your life* – doesn't help when someone answers the following question of the biker survey like this:

Question: "What is the biggest threat to a biker's safety?"

Answer: "Me!"

If it were not so true, bikers would find some humor in there.

Knowing why non-bikers spew so much venom toward bikers doesn't salve the sting of their sarcasm in referring to our ponies as *murder*cycles and us as *suicide* jockeys.

One non-biker answered almost all of the questions of the survey with three words: "Heaven can wait!"

Truth is the only things that cause fear in bikers are non-bikers!

Hunter Thompson stated the obvious:

> *Nearly everyone who has ridden a bike for any length of time will agree. The highways are crowded with people who drive as if their sole purpose in getting behind the wheel is to avenge every wrong ever done them by man, beast or fate. The only thing that keeps them in line is their own fear of death, jail and lawsuits... A bike is totally*

> *vulnerable; its only defense is maneuverability, and every accident situation is potentially fatal...*

Again, I stress the biggest problems are the "caged animals" whose aggressively bestial behavior is unleashed on bikers!

Bikers are cursed by non-bikers who transfer their jealousy and lust for control to them.

Yet bikers continue to ride because the rewards outweigh the risks; or as Christians like to say, "The crown is worth the cross."

Or as Ralph Ellison said, "Life is to be lived, not controlled, and humanity is won by continuing to play in face of certain defeat."

I like how Karen Larsen put it in *Breaking the Limit: One Woman's Motorcycle Journey Through North America* (2004):

> *"Aren't you afraid?"*
>
> *Sometimes when people asked, I suspected that they had seen too little. Their question sprang from a provincial sense of safety at home and from a fear of the unknown. Who knows what dangers exist out there? Stay home. Stay safe.*
>
> *"Aren't you afraid?"*
>
> *Sometimes when people asked, I suspected that they had seen too much. Their question transferred their fear... onto me... You might*

get hurt. You might get killed. Stay home. Stay safe.

"Aren't you afraid?"

The question seemed to transcend age, gender, race, and class...

"Aren't you afraid?"

I suppose it is a natural question...

Yes, it's *natural!*

It's *natural* to be my-way-or-the-highway.

It's *natural* to want everyone to see and do things our way.

And it's *natural* to want and try to impose our *will* on everybody else.

That's the curse!

I can't think of many groups more illustrative of that fallen tragedy than non-bikers in their deadly intentions for bikers.

I'm not suggesting there aren't some bikers who are as "fallen" as non-bikers; and

I'm not suggesting all non-bikers are curses.

I am saying there are enough bad non-bikers that bikers must take notice and ride accordingly.

Maybe that's why so many bikers ride in packs.

Maybe that's why so many bikers carry blades or heat.

Candidly, some bastard bikers give a bad name to the rest of us.

Comparatively, there are probably as many bikers as non-bikers who give bad names to their primary constituencies.

My favorite bad biker example is the obnoxiously insulting and *hopefully* ignorant use of the Confederate flag and Nazi symbols by a relatively few bikers.

When anybody other than a cracker sees a Confederate flag, they're thinking KKK, Aryan Nation, and hate groups like them.

When Jews see Nazi symbols, they think Hitler and assholes from the depths of hell who think like him.

Yeah, I know those same bikers with their Confederate and Nazi shit on their leathers would stomp anybody burning an American flag; but I learned long ago that two wrongs don't equal righteousness.

It's time for bikers, bike manufacturers, biker magazines, biker books, and biker catalogue salespeople to cut that shit out of our culture.

Lenny Mandel delivered me from my delusions about thinking such shit is nostalgic (Hey, dude, it's a memorabilia thing from WWII vets!) or cute (Oh, man, I love dem Confederate flag bikinis on a hot redneck!) in *From Cross to Cross: The Musings of a Jewish Boy Riding His Motorcycle through the Christian World* (2005):

> *I truly understand why... the swastikas they wore were trophies... spoils of war, trophies, and medals that they themselves ripped from the uniforms of their defeated foes...*
>
> *None of these trophies was any different from the scalps that the Indians shaved off of their enemies' heads and displayed*

proudly on their belts. These were badges of courage and honor...

Well, it's not the 1940s, and those "trophies" from WWII... are still vivid reminders of an horrific time. They remind us of an era where insanity reigned and where murder, torture and greed were the credo...

It's no longer a badge of honor, nor is it a trophy. No, now it is a "screw you." It's a way to show the world that they don't care about anything... So what the hell is... [a biker]... doing wearing a swastika? Does he think it's cool, that he looks tough, that it instills fear in people, or is he just stupid?

Mandel's last question is rhetorical.

It's stupid, sinful, ugly, inhuman, demonic, and other synonyms expressing the most depraved traits of fallen humanity!

And while noting my bias for authentic bikers, some bikers as well as non-bikers are not immune to that damned for damning disease.

Yes, authentics have always been cursed.

Moses.

Jesus.

Bonhoeffer.

King.

And what kept them authentic was they did not become a part of the curse.

They did not get into pissing contests with skunks.

They did not try to reason with the irrational because that's illogical.

They persisted in being authentic.

They sought to be a part of the cure to the curses.

Cures

I learned a lot with my dog at obedience school.

Our teacher said, "If your dog barks at you, don't give any treats to him, turn your back, fold your arms, and pay no attention to him until he behaves better."

He also said, "Don't praise your dog and give treats to him unless he does what's right."

My favorite Special Olympics World Golf Champion comes to mind.

Playing the back nine of one of my two favorite local golf courses, I was not having a stellar round.

I hit one of the most God-awful tee balls of my life on the 15th; and Billy said, "At least it's not in the woods."

I hit one of the best drives of my life on the 16th; and Billy said, "That makes up for the last one!"

These pages are about biker culture as metaphor and challenge to the church; and Kopper and Billy provide metaphors for curing the curses for a safe ride to our immediate and ultimate destinations.

Immediately, we determine a great deal of how the ride will go.

Farmers put it this way: "The biggest troublemaker you'll probably ever have to encounter is the one who's watching you from the mirror in the morning."

Or as one of my regular riding buddies likes to say, "There's no reason to crash and burn if you're riding safely and cautiously."

Again, those farmers got it right: "If you find yourself in a hole, the first thing to do is stop digging!"

Or as another regular riding buddy said about challenging other machines on the road, "Do not get in the face of anyone driving anything bigger and badder!"

That's my way of saying just a little common sense keeps us on top rather than underground.

Let me put it another way.

I may not be able to change the behaviors of "cagers" who make the ride so perilous so often, *but I can change how I navigate around 'em.*

My cardinal rule for safe riding is simple: "Don't expect any consideration from cagers, assume the worst, and then you'll wake up and ride again tomorrow!"

I've got a few others:

1. Take a motorcycle safety course before getting on a bike for the first time, second time, third time, or whenever;

2. Read the owner's manual of your bike *thoroughly;*

3. Talk to experienced bikers as often as possible about riding; and

4. Carry the numbers of your favorite dealership and lawyer with you at all times.

It's like my championship golfer daddy always liked to say when I was hitting the links for the first time, "You'll be surprised how lucky you get by preparing more often."

Of course, you've probably figured out by now that I'm a Christian pastor; and while the two don't always go together these days, I really believe Jesus' promise, "Come to me, all of you who are weary and burdened, and I will take care of you."

Here's the catch as revealed in His rhetorical question, "Do you want to be safe?"

It's the major lesson from our friends at AA: "Do your best and leave the rest to God!"

A friend in Tennessee wrote, "When I was stationed at Fort Riley, Kansas, my next door neighbor offered me a ride on his bike. I thought he was going to take me; but he just put me on the bike and said, 'Go!'"

He went!

Continuing to report, he continued, "Needless to say, before I got back home, I had dumped the bike once and broke a turn signal. When I got back, I offered to pay for the damage, but John was a patient, forgiving sort; and he said something that has stuck with me ever since: 'There are only two types of riders, those who have fallen and those who are going to again.'"

That's not what bikers want to hear; and that's not what the family and friends of bikers want to hear.

But it's the truth!

I was buying a helmet for my city treks; confessing how I don't like wearing 'em; and the saleswoman quipped, "It's not a question of *if* you're gonna crash but *when...* "

I've had four accidents on bikes: (1) The first day I bought one, I just jumped on without any instructions, didn't negotiate the first turn, and flew into the forest; (2) I dumped on a patch of ice while turning around the corner while leaving Speer Library at Princeton Theological Seminary; (3) I dumped after turning on my left turn signal and forgetting to put up the kickstand; and (4) I dumped as I discovered Harleys weigh a lot more than Hondas.

Call me lucky, blessed, graced, or whatever works for you, it's been a long time since my last accident because I'm more prepared this time around.

But knowing my best preparations may not protect me from the aggressive, antagonistic, or careless behaviors of cagers, I've taken to the counsel of my friend from Tennessee about falling and getting back up: "I have come to understand that bikers and Christians have at least one thing in common. We both fall; and sometimes it really hurts. The big difference is Christians have Someone who is always ready to help us back up."

Again, we try to do what's right and do better than last time; but sometimes it's beyond our control.

That's why authentics have come to understand the wisdom of yielding immediate as well as ultimate control to Him.

I'm all for those bike blessings that punctuate so many rallies; because it's no fun to break down in the sticks or blow a tire at 70 mph.

But I'm most concerned with bikers allowing themselves to be blessed by the only One who is always concerned about their immediate and ultimate safety.

My favorite devotional writer from Oklahoma Ella Jane nailed it:

> *Sometimes our situation, at best, can be described as this... We are undersized. The task is enormous and our enemies are fierce and strong. There is not enough of us to go up against them. Our calling seems greater than we can handle; leaving us feeling puny, helpless, and despondent. To make matters worse, we are surrounded on every side by those who are assigned by hell to stop us, hinder us, and attack our calling and commission. But we must never forget this one thing: "Greater is He Who is in us than he that is in the world! If God be for us, then who can be against us?"*

While it's true that bikers, even faith-filled ones, aren't immune to the meanness, madness, and misery of life in the modern world just like everybody else, bikers can ask

Him and His to ride with ‘em to increase those immediate and ultimate margins of safety.

Though it’s always best to stop digging when you’re in a hole, joining hands with Him and His reminds me of the two rabbits being chased by foxes.

They jump into a hole and one cries, “What’ll we do? There are so many of ‘em out there!”

Calmly, the other one says, “We’ll just stay in this hole together until we outnumber ‘em.”

The cure to the curses is unity – with each other as we turn to Him as the best Road Captain for our immediate and ultimate destinations.

Robert R. Kopp

Freedom

Martin Luther King, Jr. has always been one of my heroes; primarily as a champion of freedom for all who understand that the ultimate freedom fighter is Jesus: "If you stay with me, you will know the truth; and the truth will set you free."

Surely, the supreme purpose of Jesus was/is to enable confident living in the assurance of eternal life; and anyone who really believes in the eternal life that He has enabled by His sacrificial life on the cross, glorious resurrection, and reign with Father and Spirit as God isn't *that* worked up and worried about what happens the first nano-second after the last breath to this life.

Unfortunately, some folks seem to be so obsessed with that pie-in-the-sky that they miss His promise for here and now before the hereafter: "I have come that you may have life and have it abundantly!"

When authentics talk about the good news of Jesus, they mean there's nothing to worry about *after life* and this life can be a lot better even through the *mean*time by staying close to Him.

But, of course, it's like bikes.

You never know until you mount up!

Be that as it can be, my favorite sermon of all time is King's last; which he preached on the night before his assassination in Memphis, Tennessee at the Masonic Temple (April 3, 1968).

Whenever I'm feeling down and almost out, I go back to those lines that I quoted earlier as part of my *Clarification* (page 8); and whenever I need to remind myself why I ride and why others need to ride whatever enables their freedom, I go back to a few earlier sentences in that same sermon:

> *The masses of people are rising up. And wherever they are assembled today, whether they are in Johannesburg, South Africa; Nairobi Kenya; Accra, Ghana; New York City; Atlanta, Georgia; Jackson, Mississippi; or Memphis, Tennessee – the cry is always the same – "We want to be free."*

He echoed the refrain that he first uttered five years earlier at the Lincoln Memorial in Washington, D.C. (August 28, 1963) that is deep within the souls of anyone who ever wanted to ride:

> *Let freedom ring!... From every mountainside, let freedom ring!... And when this happens, and when we allow freedom to ring, when we let it ring from every village and hamlet, from every state and every city, we will be able to speed up that day when all God's children, black men and white men, Jews and gentiles, Protestants and Catholics, will be able to join hands and sing in the words of the old Negro spiritual: "Free at last! Free at last! Thank God Almighty! We are free at last!"*

Yes!

People want to be free.

Only the spiritually deaf and blind of all ages and eras were not stirred to cry out and risk personal and vocational securities for freedom as William Wallace addressed his outnumbered countrymen in the face of the superior numbers and tactical sophistication of Longshanks and his army in that powerful scene in *Braveheart* (1995) that heralds humanity's greatest aspiration:

> Old Scot: "We... [Scots]... didn't come here to fight for them... "[Scottish nobles who often sold out their countrymen for lands and titles from England].
>
> Young Scot: "Home! The English are too many!"
>
> William Wallace: "Sons of Scotland! I am William Wallace!"
>
> Young Scot: "William Wallace is seven feet tall!"
>
> William Wallace: "Yes, I've heard. Kills men by the hundreds. And if he were here, he'd consume the English with fireballs from his eyes, and bolts of lightning from his arse."
>
> *The Scottish army cheers and laughs and cheers!*
>
> William Wallace: "I *am* William Wallace! And I see a whole army of my countrymen here in defiance of tyranny. You've come to fight as free men! And free men you are! What will you do with that freedom? Will you fight?"
>
> Old Scot: "Fight? Against that? No! We will run. And we will live."
>
> William Wallace: "Aye, fight and you may die. Run and you will live... at least a while. And dying

> in your beds, many years from now, would you be willing to trade all the days, from this day to that, for one chance, just one chance, to come back here and tell our enemies that they may take our lives, but they'll never take our freedom!"

The Scottish army cheers!

What is freedom?

My young son and emerging biker Matthew says, "Freedom is when no one bothers you."

Most would agree freedom happens when the chains that bind are broken and you emerge from the cocoon like a butterfly to be who you want *and were destined* to be.

Most would agree freedom is determining, designing, and riding to your own destiny.

Most would agree freedom is taking care of yourself by rules that you've adopted for yourself rather than being taken care of by others who impose their rules upon you.

Most would agree, to borrow a phrase, freedom is "being all you can be" without someone dictating your potential and opportunities.

Freedom is choosing who you will be and what you will do and where you're going and who will be invited to ride with you.

That's why William Wallace scoffed at the Scottish nobles who thought lands, riches, and titles were worth forfeiting their freedom to the state (viz., England): "It's all for nothing if you don't have freedom."

Admittedly, as Garripoli lamented, "Cruising isn't for everyone – but then, neither is freedom."

I will never forget a startling exchange between three young girls before Senators McCain and Obama faced off for the Presidency. The girls dropped by to say hello and drop off some cookies that they made for me because, well, uh, geez, I guess they kinda like me.

I asked, "If you could vote next week, who would you vote for?"

Spontaneously and simultaneously, they screamed, "Obama! Obama!"

Without tipping my political leanings on that one because I hadn't eaten the cookies yet, I asked, "Why?"

Spontaneously and simultaneously, they said in a rather serious way for their ages, "Because he will take care of us."

That's not freedom.

That's not independence.

That's dependence.

That's offering our collar to someone else's chain.

That's the genesis of socialism.

Getting back to helmets, the bottom line for bikers is not safety.

The bottom line is freedom.

The bottom line is not yielding freedom to someone who thinks she or he knows so much better that they can dictate your beliefs and behaviors.

It's so anti-American.

That's why bikers are trying to hold the line on helmets as a patriotic act; knowing it's a terribly slippery slope to state control over every part of your life.

That's what pro-lifers have been saying for years. If any part of life is devalued, it won't be too long before other parts of life are devalued. Specifically, if you can devalue life in the womb, it won't be too long before those in control will decide *for you* that your life is no longer worth living.

That's why bikers are so patriotic.

Bikers believe America is about freedom of expression, experience, and choosing destinies.

It's Biblical.

Joshua said, "Choose this day whom you will serve!"

Jesus said, "I stand at the door and knock."

The Biblical witness is to God allowing us the choice of aligning ourselves with Him or distancing ourselves from Him.

Unmistakably, people who have chosen to side with Him and embrace His order and ethics have consistently testified to the benefits of that choice.

Biblical freedom, which I believe is what all authentic bikers and churchgoers embrace, is not doing whatever the hell you want to do *but rather being who He made you to be which will never insult His holiness nor injure anyone else.*

Biblical freedom encourages us to be His best for our lives with the thought, time, talents, and treasures that He has entrusted to us that will always honor Him and never hurt any of His as expressed and experienced.

William Stacy Johnson explained Biblical freedom in *John Calvin, Reformer for the 21st Century* (2009):

> *First, true freedom is the freedom to be what we were created to be. Human beings are made in the image of God... anything that distorts that image is sin, which is not freedom but enslavement... True freedom happens when we are freed from sin enabling us to be free for service to God and others...*
>
> *Second, because we are created by our Creator to be free ourselves, it is incumbent*

> *upon us not to bind the freedom of conscience of others... This means that our consciences should be shaped by the values and priorities of God and not by those who would distract us from God, including those in authority over us, our government, or even the church...*
>
> *The point is an important one: people are created with God-given powers of perception and discernment. Their opinions, judgments, and decisions matter. There is even a sense in which people's decision-making power is sacred...*

Again, authentics understand freedom is not about doing whatever, whenever, and with whomever; but rather freedom is the unfettered expression and experience of being who God enabled you to be which always honors Him and never hurts anyone else because God defines His essential character as love which is always laboring for the best for others without regard to who, what, where, or when without the need or expectation for response, regard, or reward.

Simply, Biblical freedom can be summed up rather concisely: "*Live* and *let live!*"

William Wallace understood our freedom as a divine right: "Your heart is free. Have the courage to follow it."

The second part of Wallace's understanding of freedom is the rub: "Have the courage to follow it."

That's what prompted him to warn, "Every man dies, not every man lives."

It's like that scene in *Wild Hogs* that prompts their fresh pursuit of freedom:

Doug: “Did you ever wake up one morning and wonder what happened to your life?”

Woody nods his head in agreement.

Doug: “All of a sudden, I’m a suburban dentist.”

Epicurus observed, “The fool does not so much live as always get ready to live. And then one day it is too late.”

I often caution churchgoers about waiting too long to be and do what our Lord invites, enables, and expects us to do *now* before it’s too late: “Someday everybody is going to return from the cemetery but you!”

“If you wait,” an old biker said a few years ago to me when I said I just wanna ride, “all that happens is that you get older.”

Peter F. Hummel ended *Motorcycles, Christians, and Heathens* (2005) with the same sentiment:

> *Life is not a rehearsal, you don’t get a second chance. My advice is to indulge, if that is the right word, with moderation but all due enthusiasm to engage in all the often repressed urges and live the secret dreams before it’s too late.*

Jesus told us to ride with Him and turn the trickles of our lives into rivers of living water.

Jesus wanted us to be who He with Father and Spirit created us to be (rivers of living water) rather than be chained to the controlling images of others (trickles).

Jesus told us to invite others to ride with us.

Bikers understand all about that; and because too many "churches" have not done that, bikers have started their own *churches*.

Bikers know that deep within the soul and gut of everyone is a desire and need to be free; and when bikers say they want to be left alone to be free, they are saying they will leave others alone who want to be free.

Yes, I am with the Christian Motorcyclists Association when it says Jesus would be a biker today.

I believe He'd load up His mule with a motor!

I believe He'd pattern a freedom that guarantees emotional, intellectual, spiritual, and even physical welfare!

He did.

He would.

He still does!

Authentics on bikes *or whatever else they're riding to freedom* do it too.

Join the chorus!

I just wanna ride!

FTW!

Robert R. Kopp

About the Author

Counting time in the womb which I always do because God does, I'm probably approaching 60 as you read this; and considering the apostle's counsel in 1 Corinthians 1:18-25, my academic and professional credentials don't mean much to authentics which is why I'm not gonna list 'em now.

Knowing some folks are obsessed with a lotta stuff that doesn't matter much *in the end,* you can read about that kinda stuff via www.belvpresbyterian.org or www.koppdisclosure.com or read pages 234-235 of *Fifteen Secrets for Life and Ministry* which never threatened Rick Warren's publishing empire.

What matters to me most these days is being authentic to who I am according to Him and hanging out with authentics who hit golf balls, ride bikes, or even gather in churches.

Currently, I'm pastor of First Presbyterian Church in Belvidere, Illinois which we call *Our Family of Faith,* professor of preaching at Carolina Evangelical Divinity School now and then, police chaplain for the community and county, and president of a junior tackle football league.

I'm also an under-achieving husband and father.

I ride a 2005 Harley-Davidson Road King.

I covet a...

I thought I was going to get one for my 30th anniversary as a pastor.

I was wrong on that.

As you read the preceding, you will discover I'm wrong about a lot of things.

CPSIA information can be obtained at www.ICGtesting.com
Printed in the USA
LVOW062152291012

304940LV00001B/120/P

9 781618 760029